GLOUCESTERSHIRE'S
FORGOTTEN BATTLE

NIBLEY GREEN
1470

GLOUCESTERSHIRE'S
FORGOTTEN BATTLE

NIBLEY GREEN
1470

PETER FLEMING & MICHAEL WOOD

TEMPUS

First published 2003

PUBLISHED IN THE UNITED KINGDOM BY:
Tempus Publishing Ltd
The Mill, Brimscombe Port
Stroud, Gloucestershire GL5 2QG

PUBLISHED IN THE UNITED STATES OF AMERICA BY:
Tempus Publishing Inc.
2 Cumberland Street
Charleston, SC 29401

British Library Cataloguing in Publication Data.
A catalogue record for this book is available from the British Library.

ISBN 0 7524 2347 9

Typesetting and origination by Tempus Publishing.
Printed in Great Britain by Midway Colour Print, Wiltshire

CONTENTS

ILLUSTRATION LIST

All illustrations courtesy of Michael Wood unless otherwise stated.

1.   Nibley Green and the Tyndale Monument.
2.   Bristol Cathedral gatehouse.
3 & 4. Gatehouse inscription.
5.   Berkeley Castle.
6.   A Berkeley effigy in Bristol Cathedral (copyright Dean and Chapter of Bristol, used with permission).
7.   The tomb recess of Thomas, Lord Berkeley (copyright Dean and Chapter of Bristol, used with permission).
8.   The Berkeley arms (copyright Dean and Chapter of Bristol, used with permission).
9.   A Berkeley effigy in Bristol Cathedral (copyright Dean and Chapter of Bristol, used with permission).
10.   Lord Thomas and Lady Katharine (Copyright St Mary's Church, Berkeley, used with permission).
11.   Lord Maurice and his mother Margaret (copyright Dean and Chapter of Bristol, used with permission).
12.   Richard Beauchamp (Brindley, *Richard Beauchamp*).
13.   Warwick at the siege of Caen, 1417 (Brindley, *Richard Beauchamp*).
14.   Berkeley Castle and Church.
15.   The death of Richard Beauchamp (Brindley, *Richard Beauchamp*).
16.   A genealogy from the *Beauchamp Pageant* (Brindley, *Richard Beauchamp*).
17.   James with his father James, Lord Berkeley (Copyright St Mary's Church, Berkeley, used with permission).
18.   The Great Hall, Berkeley Castle (copyright Berkeley Castle, used with permission of Mr & Mrs Berkeley).
19.   Single combat (Brindley, *Richard Beauchamp*).
20.   South-west Gloucestershire.
21.   Bristol's sheriff and two sergeants (copyright Bristol Record Office, used with permission).

COLOUR PLATES

15.   Plan of Bristol, from *The Mayor of Bristol's Kalendar* (copyright Bristol Record Office, used with permission).

16–18. Heraldic glass in the Great Hall of Berkeley Castle (copyright Berkeley Castle, used with permission of Mr & Mrs Berkeley).

19.   The inner gatehouse of Berkeley Castle (copyright Berkeley Castle, used with permission of Mr & Mrs Berkeley).

20.   'The Battle of Nibley Green', by Robert Hollingworth (courtesy of Mr & Mrs Eley, Nibley House).

21.   The sunken lane leading from Nibley Green.

22.   Grantley Berkeley's Druid Oak.

ACKNOWLEDGEMENTS

A number of individuals have given generously of their time and expertise. We are grateful to Mr and Mrs Berkeley; Mrs Halls, Berkeley Castle Custodian; Mr David Smith, the Berkeley archivist; Mr and Mrs Eley of Nibley House; Mr Mark Jones of Wotton-under-Edge; and Mr and Mrs Tandy. Our thanks are also due to the Dean and Chapter of Bristol, and the incumbents of St Martin's, North Nibley and St Mary's, Berkeley. David Smith and Professor Michael Hicks read and provided perceptive comments on early drafts of Chapters 2 and 3. Any mistakes or doubtful interpretations are, of course, ours, and not theirs.

We are grateful to the staffs of Gloucestershire and Bristol Record Offices, the Local Studies Department of Gloucester Library, the Central Reference Library at Bristol, the Gloucestershire Sites and Monuments Record, the Public Record Office, and the British Library. We also appreciate the patience and encouragement of Jonathan Reeve and Alan Sutton of Tempus.

Michael would like to thank his parents for their support, and Luisa for the hours she spent enthralled in proofreading. Peter would like to thank Ann, for her patience and support. Keith Dockray has provided inspiration, encouragement and good humour, as usual.

PREFACE

This book has its origins in a Master's Dissertation, a TV programme and a conference. The first was written by Michael, under Peter's supervision; the second was made by Available Light for HTV, and featured Peter along with Keith Dockray; the third was organised by Keith Stenner for the Richard III Society, and included contributions from Peter, Anton Bantock and Christopher Scott. All three projects had the Berkeleys and Nibley Green as their subject, and all three came at around the same time. There seemed to be sufficient scope and interest in the battle of Nibley Green to justify doing something more ambitious, and this book is the result. Michael's dissertation has provided the foundation, with additional material and archival research by Peter, who wrote Chapters 1 to 4, with Chapter 5 written by Michael. Unless otherwise stated, Michael took all of the photographs.

LIST OF ABBREVIATIONS

BL	British Library, London
Carpenter, *Locality and Polity*	C. Carpenter, *Locality and Polity: A Study of Warwickshire Landed Society, 1401–1499* (Cambridge, 1992)
CCR	*Calendar of Close Rolls*
CFR	*Calendar of Fine Rolls*
CPR	*Calendar of Patent Rolls*
Griffiths, *Henry VI*	R.A. Griffiths, *The Reign of King Henry VI: The Exercise of Royal Authority, 1422–1461* (London, 1981)
GRO	Gloucestershire Record Office, Gloucester
Hicks, *Clarence*	M.A. Hicks, *False, Fleeting, Perjur'd Clarence: George, Duke of Clarence, 1449–78* (2nd edn, Bangor, 1992)
Hicks, *Warwick*	M.A. Hicks, *Warwick the Kingmaker* (Oxford, 1998)
Jeayes, *Catalogue*	I.H. Jeayes, *Descriptive Catalogue of the Charters and Muniments... at Berkeley Castle* (Bristol, 1892)
Lives	J. Maclean (ed.), *The Berkeley Manuscripts: The Lives of the Berkeleys*, vol. 2 (Bristol and Gloucestershire Archaeological Society, 1883)
PRO	Public Record Office, Kew
Ross, *Edward IV*	C. Ross, *Edward IV* (London, 1974)
Rotuli Parliamentorum	*Rotuli Parliamentorum, 1377–1503*, 4 vols (London, 1783)
TBGAS	*Transactions of the Bristol and Gloucestershire Archaeological Society*
Wedgwood, *History of Parliament*	J.C. Wedgwood, *The History of Parliament: Biographies of the Members of the Commons House, 1439–1509* (London, 1936)

INTRODUCTION

The motorist driving along the M5 motorway a few miles north of Bristol and looking up to the rolling hills to the east, will see the slender obelisk that stands above the village of North Nibley in Gloucestershire. This monument marks the birthplace – either here or at nearby Slimbridge – of William Tyndale, the sixteenth-century Protestant martyr. But North Nibley has another, and surer – given the uncertainty over Tyndale's birthplace – claim to fame. In the fields to the south-west of the village, on 20 March 1470, two private armies clashed. The leader of one, Viscount Lisle, was killed, leaving his opponent, Lord Berkeley, victorious. The battle of Nibley Green took place during what has come to be known as the Wars of the Roses, a series of conflicts between branches of the English royal family, beginning with the challenge issued by Richard, duke of York, his sons and their Neville allies to the Lancastrian King Henry VI in the 1450s, and ending with Henry VII's establishment of the Tudor dynasty in the 1480s. Nibley Green, it must be admitted, does not rank among the great battles of these wars – indeed, the extent to which it can be seen as part of the Wars of the Roses at all is debatable – but whilst little more than a skirmish, and usually regarded as of no great importance to national politics, it does have its place in the historical record book. It is reputed to have been the last private battle fought on English soil, and was the most dramatic episode in what was probably the longest running case in English legal history, a veritable 'Jarndyce *versus* Jarndyce', worthy of a medieval *Bleak House*.

In a sense, the Berkeley dispute did indeed have its Dickens, in the person of John Smyth of North Nibley.[1] Smyth was born into a family of Lincolnshire gentry in 1567, and was educated initially at the Free School in Derby. He entered Berkeley service at the age of nine, attending upon the young Thomas, son and heir to Henry, Lord Berkeley. It was as friends that they entered Magdalen College, Oxford together. Smyth went on to the Middle Temple to study Common Law and in 1596 re-entered Berkeley service, putting his legal expertise to good use as steward. In this position Smyth had free access to the family archives in the muniment room of

1. Nibley Green, with the Tyndale Monument in the distance.

Berkeley Castle and used this to compile a detailed history of the Berkeley family from the Norman Conquest to his present. The manuscript, completed in 1618 (but with later additions) was presented to George, Lord Berkeley with the intention that it should provide him with examples, drawn from the lives of his ancestors, of good and bad conduct. It was therefore conceived as a work of moral and practical education. While Smyth dedicated almost his entire life to Berkeley service, he also saw it as his duty to be objective, and to offer to Lord Berkeley a 'warts and all' picture of his ancestors: he is particularly scathing about William, Lord Berkeley, the protagonist of Nibley Green.

To later generations, Smyth's work has provided a voluminous – if at times difficult to digest – source for the history of one of the English peerage's most ancient families. Smyth's method, in what is usually known as *The Lives of the Berkeleys*, is to deal with each lord in turn, recounting his birth, education, honours, land-holding, wives and children. This is not an easy read, perhaps, but it repays perseverance. Smyth was a tireless and thorough researcher, and his work shows not only mastery of the family archive, but also an impressive familiarity with the archives of central government, much of which were then held at the Tower of London. He was a careful historian, citing his sources in the margins of his manuscript, and often reproducing documents in full, accurately transcribed. He probably had access to family documents which have since been lost.[2] In following his tracks through the unpublished records, we have found him to be a reliable guide.

Smyth's work provided the basis for a series of ever more fanciful retellings of the story of Nibley Green until the late nineteenth century. Only then, with the emergence of history as an academic discipline, could Smyth's scholarship be properly appreciated. The pioneer in this regard was James Cooke, who in 1879 published what have been up until now the only modern treatments of the Berkeley dispute in its entirety.[3] However, while he provided a clear narrative of events, his accounts still draw heavily on Smyth, and follow him in placing the battle in the wrong year: 1469 rather than 1470. Even so, Cooke did a great service by making Smyth's version of events accessible, since the *Lives* was at that time still unpublished. This task was performed in 1883, when Sir John Maclean produced a two-volume edition of *The Lives of the Berkeleys* for the Bristol and Gloucestershire Archaeological Society, with an edition of Smyth's *Description of the Hundred of Berkeley* following the next year.[4] Finally, in 1892 Isaac Herbert Jeayes published his *Descriptive Catalogue* of the archives held in Berkeley Castle, many of which had been used by Smyth.[5]

So, by the opening of the twentieth century, everything was in place for a thorough re-evaluation of the Berkeley dispute in its national context. But this did not happen. The next substantial treatment, T.A. Ryder's *Mid-Gloucestershire Through the Ages*, published in 1951, included a chapter on the fifteenth century which largely followed Smyth and Cooke, as did Jonathan Blow's article in *History Today*, 'Nibley Green, 1469', which appeared the following year (as his title shows, he too was misled by Smyth's error in dating the battle).[6] Blow did make more progress in relating the dispute to the national political scene, but his misattribution of Nibley Green to 1469 made a nonsense of putting the battle itself in its proper context.

Since the 1950s, the study of fifteenth-century English political history has been revolutionised by the work of K.B. Mcfarlane and his followers. Part of their approach has been to look for the keys to understanding national politics in events in the localities, and in particular, the working out of patronage and 'good lordship' among the gentry and nobility, with their accompanying feuds and alliances. In this light, the Berkeley dispute has been seen as a useful example of what happens when things go wrong. As such, it has often appeared in passing references, almost the classic 'footnote in history'. Usually, historians have been content simply to follow Smyth and Cooke, to the extent that even eminent scholars have repeated Smyth's mis-dating of the battle. To some degree it appears that the very professionalism of Smyth as an historian has dissuaded his modern counterparts from going much beyond his account.

There have been exceptions of course, and we are happy to acknowledge our debt to those historians who have subjected episodes in the dispute to painstaking archival research, foremost among whom are Dr Bridget Harvey, Dr

Alexandra Sinclair, Professor Tony Pollard and Professor Michael Hicks. At several points our account draws heavily on their expertise. However, the present work is the first detailed reassessment of the battle itself, drawing on evidence unknown to Smyth. It is also the first attempt since Cooke to see the whole dispute – with, admittedly, much greater emphasis on its fifteenth-century phase than its later stages – in the perspective of national politics and political culture.

1

THE ROAD TO NIBLEY GREEN

Many English aristocrats have claimed that their ancestors came over with the Conqueror. In most cases such claims are, to put it at its most polite, imaginative. The Berkeleys, of whom there are still representatives in residence at Berkeley Castle, can, with a clear conscience, trump these often spurious claims. While medieval family tradition traced their origins to the King of Denmark, the truth is in a way even more impressive.[1] The Berkeleys' progenitor was in England *before* the Conquest. He was an Englishman called Eadnoth, and was a thegn and high official under Edward the Confessor. He survived 1066 and William made him responsible for the defence of Somerset, in which capacity he was killed in 1068 by the sons of Harold. Eadnoth's son, Harding, continued in the family tradition of royal service, and was a noted lawyer. The family's association with Berkeley begins with Harding's younger son, Robert. Robert fitz Harding made his fortune in Bristol, probably from its sea-borne trade, but it was in the treacherous currents of twelfth-century politics that he made his greatest mark. Service to the earls of Gloucester brought him the manors of Bedminster and Bilswick, on the outskirts of Bristol, as well as estates elsewhere in the West Country. Still more significantly, during the civil wars of 1138 to 1153 he was one of the region's leading supporters of Matilda and her son Henry against King Stephen. His association with the eventual victor in this conflict bore fruit even before Henry II's accession in 1154. The previous year Henry had granted him the Honour of Berkeley on the understanding that he would build a castle there. Berkeley had been forfeited by Roger de Berkeley, an adherent of the defeated Stephen. Robert used his children's marriages to secure his hold on the new acquisition: his son Maurice married Roger de Berkeley's daughter, who brought with her the manor of Slimbridge, and his daughter Helen married Roger de Berkeley's son and heir.

Evidence for Robert's castle at Berkeley is hard to detect: what we see today is largely a later medieval structure. A far more tangible link to the first of the

2. The twelfth-century Bristol Cathedral gatehouse, with c.1500 upper storeys.

3 and 4. An inscription on the gatehouse proclaims King Henry II and Robert fitz Harding, son of the King of Denmark, as the first founders of the abbey.

fitz Harding lords of Berkeley is to be found in Bristol. Robert founded St Augustine's Abbey, in his manor of Bilswick, in the 1140s. The abbey church now forms the east end of Bristol Cathedral; it too is largely later medieval, but the magnificent chapter house and gateway date to the second phase of building that resulted from Henry II's patronage of the abbey. Across College Green, the Lord Mayor's Chapel is all that is left of St Mark's Hospital, originally attached to St Augustine's, and refounded by a branch of the Berkeley family in the thirteenth century.

By the end of the fourteenth century the Berkeleys had established themselves as the leading magnate family in Gloucestershire.[2] The great bulk of their holdings lay within the county borders, with their core in the Honour of Berkeley, which was co-terminous with Berkeley hundred. Within a six-mile radius of Berkeley Castle lay two boroughs, Berkeley and Wotton-under-Edge, and ten manors, over which the lords of Berkeley exercised their own jurisdiction, holding the hundred court, and enjoying the profits of justice. The sheriffs of Gloucestershire had no authority in this private fiefdom: royal writs had to be addressed to the Berkeleys' officials, who would carry them out – or not – as they wished. The Berkeleys even had the right to hang felons convicted before their courts.

The hundred of Berkeley constituted one twelfth of the entire taxable wealth of the county, as measured by the fourteenth-century subsidy assessments. With their manors in north Somerset, Bristol properties, and a scattering of holdings in other counties, the Berkeleys' annual landed income around 1400 probably amounted to more than £2,000. This puts them some way ahead of the lesser nobility, and compares very well with the greatest magnates of the early fifteenth century, such as the earls of Warwick and dukes of Buckingham and York, who had annual landed incomes of between £3,500 and £4,000.[3] The family's wealth allowed for younger sons to found two cadet branches, the Berkeleys of Beverstone and the Berkeleys of Stoke

Gifford, both well-endowed with lands. The fourteenth-century Berkeleys also enjoyed political hegemony over their county. At any one time, probably half of the Gloucestershire gentry were part of the Berkeley affinity, and of those perhaps as many as a quarter were retainers.

The Berkeleys owed their early prominence to Robert fitz Harding's friendship with Henry II. His successors continued to benefit from royal patronage, but this came to an end in the 1320s when Lord Maurice rebelled against Edward II and his lands were forfeited. In 1327 the new Lord Berkeley, Thomas, joined with Edward's queen Isabella and her lover, Roger Mortimer, who was also Thomas's brother-in-law, to topple the king, and from April to September Edward was kept prisoner at Berkeley Castle. There were two attempts to rescue him – the first actually succeeded in liberating him briefly before his recapture – and after the second it was decided that he was too dangerous to be allowed to live. What happened next constitutes the most notorious episode in the history of Berkeley Castle; indeed, if there is one fact that everybody knows about the Berkeleys, it is that Edward II was murdered in their castle. Tourists can still see the cell above the castle cess-pit where, after the noxious odours had failed to kill him, he was bundled between two mattresses while a red-hot poker was thrust into his anus: or so the story goes. The king's murder allowed his son to succeed as Edward III, but the regicides still had to be punished. Mortimer was tied to a ladder and

5. Berkeley Castle.

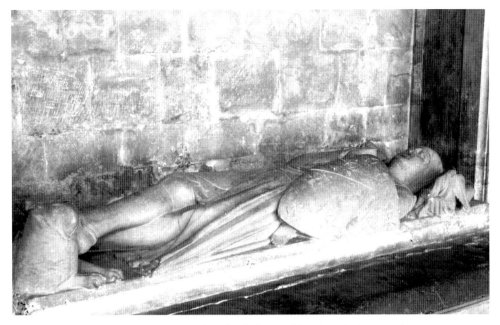

6. A Berkeley effigy in Bristol Cathedral, possibly of Lord Thomas (d. 1243).

had his beating heart ripped from his body. Lord Berkeley escaped any such punishment by claiming that at the time of the murder he was lying ill in his house at Bradley, six miles away. Had his interrogators looked at his household accounts, however, they would have seen that he did not arrive at Bradley until six days after the murder...

Twenty years later the Black Death came to Europe. In 1348/9 it ravaged England, cutting the population of some communities by half and wiping out entire families. In 1349 Lord Thomas was approaching his sixtieth year, and nearing the end of his active life: after 1350 he would take little part in public affairs, and he may have been suffering ill health until his death in 1361. With mortality all around, Thomas had to consider the consequences of his own demise. Many other landed families had disappeared in the male line because of the deaths of their sons, leaving the estates to be split up between heiresses and the family name to be lost in oblivion. Thomas sought to avoid this fate for his own family by the use of a legal device called an entail. A landowner who wished to extend his control over his land beyond his own lifetime could grant – or enfeoff – his property to a group of trustees – feoffees – who would then grant it back to him on condition that, after his death, it would not be inherited by certain categories of people. An entail was created by this means, and the conditions under which Lord Thomas's entailed lands would be inherited meant that they could pass only to a male heir. This form of entail

7. The tomb recess of Thomas, Lord Berkeley (d. 1321), seen from the Berkeley Chapel, Bristol Cathedral. The polygonal stellate arch is a characteristic feature of Berkeley architectural patronage.

8. The Berkeley arms (extreme left and right of the panel) in the Berkeley Chapel.

was known as tail male. In 1349 Thomas entailed, in tail male, the castle, manor and hundred of Berkeley, the manors of Alkington, Appleridge, Cam, Cowley, Ham, Hinton, Hurst, Slimbridge, Simondshall, Wotton-under-Edge and Upton St Leonards (all but the last within the hundred and honour of Berkeley), the advowsons (the right of patronage over a church, meaning that its possessor could effectively choose the incumbent) of Wotton and Slimbridge, twenty-two marks of annual rent from Frampton-on-Severn, and the manor and hundred of Portbury in Somerset.[4] While there was much else left unentailed, these properties formed the core of the Berkeley estate, and henceforth, they ought only to descend through the male line. By this means, Thomas intended that there should always be a Berkeley in Berkeley Castle. The 1349 entail was one of the roots of the longest-running dispute in English legal history.

These precautions were not needed after Thomas's death. His son Maurice lived to succeed him in 1361, despite having sustained serious wounds at the battle of Poitiers in 1356, which left him an invalid for the rest of his life. He too left a son and heir, another Thomas, although at his accession in 1368 he still had another six years of his minority left to run. This Lord Thomas gave

9. A Berkeley effigy in Bristol Cathedral, possibly of Lord Maurice (d. 1326).

10. Lord Thomas (d. 1361) and Lady Katherine, St Mary's Church, Berkeley.

valuable support to Henry Bolingbroke when he challenged Richard II for the throne in 1399, and reaped the rewards when the usurper became Henry IV. At Thomas's death in 1417, Berkeley fortunes had reached their height.

Thomas had used the profits of royal patronage to acquire further property, including a London mansion and estates around Berkeley and Portbury, but the single most important addition – albeit short-lived – came through marriage. A year before his death, Maurice had entered into negotiations with Gerrard de Warren, heir to the Lisle lands of his father and the Tyes lands of his mother, with the purpose of marrying Warren's daughter Margaret to his son Thomas. A four-year delay was agreed because of the youth of the couple (Margaret was only seven), but Maurice's rapidly failing health meant that the marriage was brought forward, and the couple were married in November 1367.[5] Gerrard de Warren died in 1382, leaving Margaret as his sole heir, and so she brought to her husband the huge Lisle-Tyes inheritance of twenty manors and other properties in seven counties. In the early fifteenth century this estate was valued at around £600 *per annum*.[6] The lure of the Lisle-Tyes estate brought about one further dynastic coup. Thomas and Margaret had only one child, a daughter. With Margaret's death in March 1392 that daughter, Elizabeth, became the Lisle-Tyes heiress. Her father might marry again and produce a son and heir, so Elizabeth's prospective husband could

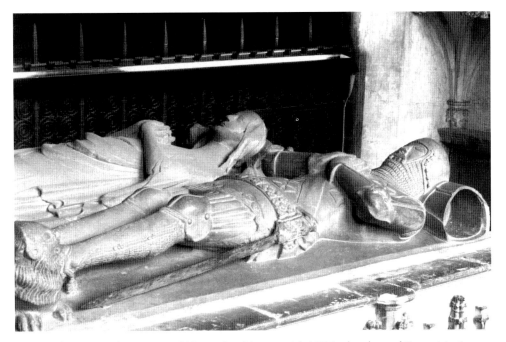

11. Lord Maurice (d. 1368), and his mother Margaret (d. 1357), daughter of Roger Mortimer, earl of March and first wife of Lord Thomas (d. 1361), Bristol Cathedral.

only count on acquiring her maternal inheritance. That was inducement enough. Within six months of her mother's death Elizabeth had married one of England's most eligible – in terms of wealth and political prospects at least – bachelors in England: Richard Beauchamp, heir to the earldom of Warwick.[7] The Beauchamp alliance was another root of the great Berkeley law suit.

Lord Thomas did not marry again. Smyth claims that

> The greef of [Margaret's] death soe fastened upon the affections of her lord and husband, that hee never after affected marriage, although he was at her death but thirty eight years of age, and of able constitution, and then without male issue to uphold his name and barony.[8]

As it became clear to the Beauchamps that Thomas would not seek another wife, they may have looked forward to the delightful prospect of Richard inheriting the entire Berkeley estate. But by the terms of the 1349 entail this should not have happened, for the heir to the Berkeley lands entailed in tail male was James, nephew of Lord Thomas.[9] Thomas, however, did not always make this clear to all interested parties. He seems to have acknowledged the entail when it suited him, as when marriages were being negotiated for James and his brother Maurice, but not when it came to courting the Beauchamps' favour. Thomas himself may have attempted to break the entail in order to give himself more room to manoeuvre. Less than a month before his death he enfeoffed a number of the entailed lands with others held in fee simple without any differentiation, and no mention of the condition applying to the former.[10] Smyth suggests several possible reasons for his behaviour. Perhaps he could not decide 'betweene name and nature', that is, between preserving the Berkeley name in the male line, or giving his only child what would have been hers if the laws of inheritance had been allowed to take their course. More cynically, Smyth suggests that by preserving this uncertainty,

> Hee would on the one side serve himselfe with the Court favour of his son in lawe, one of the most powerfull and best favored subjects of his time, loaden with honors and offices of state, And on the other side... in the same seasons make harvest of the person of his said nephewe and heire male, by a double sale of his mariage, first to Sir John St John, and after to Sir Humphrey Stafford, not sticking in those agreements to declare his said nephewe to bee heir to all his inheritance intailed.[11]

Finally, he speculates, 'That by not declareing his heire, both parties had care, if not to serve yet not to discontent him'.[12] One other possibility is that the Beauchamps were putting pressure on Thomas to disregard the entail. Even at the time of Richard Beauchamp's marriage, it might have been prudent to anticipate the possibility of Thomas dying without a son and heir, and such a contingency could have been allowed for by an agreement guaranteeing all the Berkeley estates to Elizabeth. Even had this not been the case, a similar concession might have been pressed upon Thomas when it became clear that he would remain unmarried.

Thomas Lord Berkeley died on 13 July 1417. The secret of his intentions regarding the heir to the entailed properties – if he had ever made up his mind – went with him to the grave. The only indication we have of his last will is a copy of his testament, the document which concerns itself with the deceased's pious and charitable bequests and with the disposal of his or her moveables. His last will proper, the *ultima voluntas* that would have dealt with his landed property, does not seem to have survived, assuming that one ever existed. When he died he was attended by his daughter Elizabeth and her husband Richard Beauchamp, since 1401 earl of Warwick. Unfortunately for him, James Berkeley was in Dorset, staying with his in-laws. Elizabeth and Richard seized Thomas's papers immediately after he was dead – William,

In this pagent is shewed howe the noble Erle Richard was made knyght
of the Garter at that tyme to his grete worship. And after by mancull
act by hym ful notably and knyghtly acheved in his pore person did
grete hono' & worship to the noble ordre of knyghtes of the Garter
as by the pagents hereafter folowyng more plenly is shewed.

12. Richard Beauchamp, earl of Warwick, shown being invested as a Knight of the Garter
at Shrewsbury, 1403.

Lord Berkeley would recover them after the battle of Nibley Green – and there must be the suspicion that his last will was among them, and contained matter not to the couple's liking.[13] What does survive has a certain interest but is unenlightening on the point at issue. By his testament he left to his daughter his best pair of morning mittens and a silver bowl containing £20; to his nephew went his best bed, his great bowl of jet, and twenty complete harnesses of armour and as many lances.[14] These last, at least, James would find a use for over the coming years.

Within days of Thomas's death Warwick was called away to muster his retinue for campaign in France, and Henry V committed the Berkeley estates to three of the earl's officials until the rightful heir could be ascertained. Right from the start, Warwick's closeness to the king, and his important role as a leader in the French war, meant that there was little likelihood of James receiving fair treatment from the crown or its officials. James's problems were exacerbated by the fact that the king had ordered the suspension of all suits against the earl during his frequent absences in France. Despite all this, James was taking steps to secure his inheritance. On the decease of a tenant-in-chief like Lord Berkeley, who held lands directly of the king, an enquiry, called an inquisition *post mortem*, was held by the escheators (crown financial officers) in each county in which he had property, to determine who were his rightful heirs. The process was put in train by the procurement from the royal admin-istration of a writ of *diem clausit extremum*. In cases where the succession was disputed, it was in the interests of rival claimants to apply for these writs as soon as possible so that they had a greater chance of influencing the findings of the inquisitions in their favour. This is what James did, suing out a writ of *diem clausit extremum* directed to the Gloucestershire escheator. Countess Elizabeth attempted to delay the inquisitions, then to bribe and cajole the jurors, the under-sheriff and even the escheator. Her attempts to subvert the legal process strongly suggest that she was well aware of the existence of the 1349 entail. Despite her best efforts, at the inquisition which opened at Gloucester on 27 September 1417, the jury eventually found, after over two months of delays, that James was indeed heir to his uncle's entailed property.[15]

A legal judgement means nothing until it is enforced, and the Beauchamps refused to recognise the verdict or to surrender the entailed properties. They were massively more powerful than their opponent. James Berkeley was a young man, having just attained his majority, and deprived of access to his inheritance had little to offer his uncle's former retainers, most of whom trans-ferred their allegiance to the earl and countess of Warwick. Berkeley's retainers had, after all, been used to the patronage of a lord whose estates spread over

13. Warwick at the siege of Caen, 1417.

much of southern England: why should they throw in their lot with his relatively impoverished nephew, when they could enjoy the largesse of his daughter, who could spend as much as £1,000 a year on her household?[16] However, a few remained loyal to James, allowing him to mount sporadic attacks on Beauchamp servants and property while also participating in largely unsuccessful attempts to achieve an arbitrated settlement.

James could also count on help from his father-in-law, Sir Humphrey Stafford. While of no great influence himself, Sir Humphrey was a member of the affinity of Henry V's younger brother, Humphrey, duke of Gloucester. This link would prove decisive, for James was now able to attract the patronage of one of the mightiest in the land: mightier even than the earl of Warwick. Gloucester was not a man noted for his altruism, and in return for the duke's support James had to promise that as soon as he took possession of his inheritance he would grant his new patron 1,000 marks and the reversion in fee simple of lands to the annual value of 400 marks. Gloucester eventually proved his worth. While Henry V was in France, his brothers Gloucester and John, duke of Bedford, shared the lieutenancy of England. In May 1420 Bedford left to join his royal brother in Paris and Gloucester began one of his periods as lieutenant. In September 1421, nearly a year after their agreement, the king granted James's petition, seconded by the duke, to be allowed to sue his livery to the entailed property, which meant that he had official approval to enter his inheritance, but this still had to be enforced. This proved impossible until the Beauchamps received an order from the king himself to surrender the disputed properties; faced with the threat of royal disfavour, they backed down, and James was at last able to take possession of his lands. This probably occurred between May 1422, when Gloucester was once again appointed lieutenant, and the end of August. In early September James was able to enfeoff some of the disputed properties as security for payment of the 1,000 marks he had promised to Gloucester for his assistance. By contrast, Bedford had been vigorously courted by the Beauchamps, and when James had petitioned parliament in December 1421, during one of his lieutenancies, nothing had been done.

Lord James was not allowed to enjoy his inheritance in peace. Henry V died on 31 August 1422. Early the following month the Beauchamps, in the words of Smyth,

> ...laid about the... Castle of Berkeley great multitude of people in maner of warre; In which time were many persons hurt and maymed, and some slayne...[17]

Both sides imported men from the Forest of Dean, and the countess also used Beauchamp followers from outside the county, resulting in a good deal of disruption and lawlessness in this part of Gloucestershire.

Bishop Morgan of Worcester, whose diocese included Gloucestershire, rode to Berkeley Castle and persuaded the assailants to lift the siege.[18] He then persuaded Berkeley and Warwick to agree to arbitration, which he subsequently led. His fellow arbiters were Sir John Tiptoft, William Babington, a justice of the court of common pleas, and William Cheyne, a justice of King's Bench. All three were already known to the contending parties, having attempted to arbitrate a settlement the previous year. Bishop Morgan had brought a halt to the worst of the violence and initiated a process of negotiation which would eventually, in October 1425, bring about a temporary settlement of the dispute.

The 1425 settlement came as the culmination of a long process of patient negotiation by the bishop of Worcester, putting into practice the imperative on ecclesiastics to bring peace to their communities, but was made possible by Warwick's changing circumstances. Countess Elizabeth had died in December 1422, and within a year Warwick had married Isabel, widow of his cousin Richard Beauchamp of Worcester, and heir to the vast Despenser estate. A son followed in March 1425. With his new family the Berkeley inheritance lost

14. View of Berkeley Castle and Church: church and detached tower to the left and castle to the right.

some of its importance, and his son and heir made the endowment of his three daughters by Elizabeth less of a priority. The earl was also distracted by fresh campaigning in France. In addition, 1425 was a year in which Gloucester enjoyed political ascendancy in England, making it easier for him to enforce a settlement on the Beauchamps.

Under the terms of the settlement, Warwick received the entailed properties of Wotton, Cowley, Simondshall, the manor and hundred of Portbury, and rents in Frampton-on-Severn and Slimbridge, to hold for life, and he was confirmed in his possession of the unentailed properties. This left James with Berkeley Castle, Alkington, Appleridge, Cam, Ham, Hinton, Hurst, Slimbridge and Upton St Leonards, together with a reversionary interest in Warwick's entailed lands, which meant that after the earl's death they would remain to James or his heirs. The peace would hold for nearly fourteen years.

Richard Beauchamp, earl of Warwick, died at Rouen on 30 April 1439. James Lord Berkeley may have spared a prayer for his soul, but is unlikely to have mourned his passing. James had known relative peace since 1425, but he had also known relative penury. As Smyth relates,

> this peace I am assured cost the lord James soe deere, having no personall estate from any of his Ancestors, and none of the portion of his first wife, that hee became much indebted; a continuall borrower, and often of small sums, and some of those upon pawnes, yea of Church vestments and Altar-goods;[19]

For nearly fourteen years James had been living with the knowledge that the entailed manors granted to Warwick, which he believed to be his by right, were being unjustly kept from him. Now, surely, he could enjoy what was his.

Warwick's Berkeley daughters had other ideas.[20] All three had married well: Elizabeth to George Nevill, Lord Latimer; Eleanor to Thomas, Lord Roos, and after his death in 1430 to Edmund Beaufort, count of Mortain, later earl of Dorset and then duke of Somerset; and Margaret to John, Lord Talbot, from 1442 earl of Shrewsbury. Latimer was the brother of Richard Nevill, earl of Salisbury, and uncle to his son and namesake the earl of Warwick, who would be known as the 'Kingmaker'; Beaufort was descended from John of Gaunt, one of the sons of Edward III, and his family enjoyed great influence about the young Henry VI; while Talbot, 'The English Achilles', had already established a reputation as one of England's most feared and effective commanders in the Hundred Years' War. Talbot had a violent temper, and could be ruthless in pursuit of his enemies, whether at home or abroad. Once again,

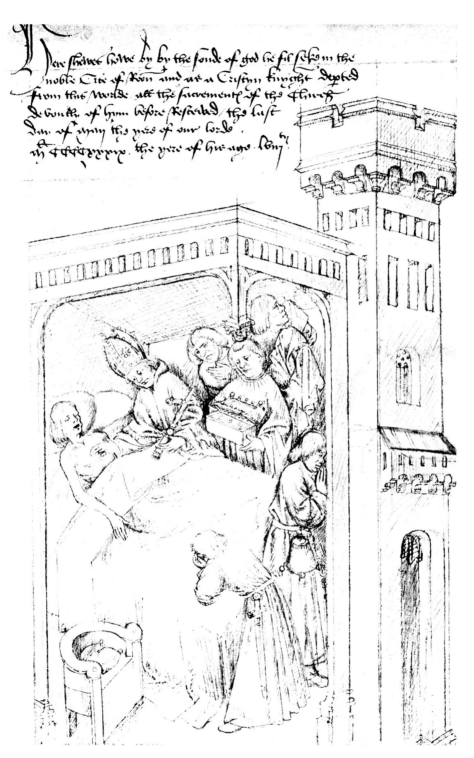

15. The death of Richard Beauchamp, earl of Warwick, in 1439.

Lord Berkeley was faced with potentially overwhelming odds. But he was not alone. As well as the continuing patronage of the duke of Gloucester – whose usefulness was declining along with his political influence – James could count on the support of his family.

He married his third wife in 1423. She was Isabel, daughter of Thomas Mowbray earl, later duke, of Norfolk, and his second wife Elizabeth, daughter of Richard, earl of Arundel, and widow of Henry Ferrers, son and heir of William, Lord Ferrers of Groby. His marriage to Isabel brought him three Norfolk manors, and lands in Essex and elsewhere, but far more important than property were the dynastic connections forged by this union.[21] Some indication of the new constellation in which he now found himself is provided by the list of feoffees on whom the entailed Berkeley estates were settled around the time of his third marriage.[22] Among them were the earl of Norfolk, Norfolk's brother-in-law, Sir Thomas, later Lord, Stanley, and Robert Wingfield, a Mowbray retainer. The identities of the rest hint at how James had made such a dazzling catch as Isabel Mowbray, so soon after gaining possession of a still troubled and uncertain inheritance. They were his patron, Humphrey duke of Gloucester; the duke's associate, John Holand, earl of Huntingdon, Henry IV's nephew, who six years later would become a royal councillor; and Bishop Morgan of Worcester, who had extricated James from the siege of Berkeley Castle.[23] By 1439 Gloucester's influence at court was virtually at an end, although he would remain an irritant to the dominant Beaufort faction until his death in 1447. On the other hand, while Thomas, duke of Norfolk had died in 1432, his successors and their associates would remain significant Berkeley allies for decades to come, as would the Stanleys.

Smyth found Isabel Mowbray entirely admirable:

> Shee was a lady of great vertue, entirely lovinge her husband, and the children shee had by him; And in their distresses the principall stay and follower of their sutes and buisinesses;[24]

He had a very different opinion of William, the eldest son of James and Isabel, as we shall see, but for a time at least, he was a valuable support to his parents. William was born in 1426. Even as young as thirteen, he proved politically useful to his parents: the month after Warwick's death he was part of Cardinal Beaufort's household at Calais, where he was attending a peace conference.[25] Placing their eldest son into the Cardinal's household was an inspired move by the Berkeleys: as Gloucester's star waned, they were seeking the good lordship

16. A genealogy from the *Beauchamp Pageant* showing Warwick's marriages to Elizabeth, daughter of Lord Berkeley, and Isabel Despenser. The daughters of the first marriage, Margaret, Eleanor and Elizabeth, are shown on the left-hand side, Henry, duke of Warwick and Anne, wife of Richard Neville, earl of Warwick, children of the second marriage, to the right.

of his rival, who was very much in the ascendant at court. It was just as well that James and Isabel were politically astute: they would need every ounce of this quality in the trials that would soon follow.

As soon as he heard of the earl's death James seized possession of the entailed properties which had been conceded to Warwick by the 1425 settlement. However, on 2 July he was committed to the Tower, from which he would only be released after entering into a recognisance of £1,000, a sum he would lose if he did not appear in Chancery at Michaelmas (29 September) for the next three years. Whether or not he had observed the necessary legal niceties in the process of recovering the former Warwick manors is beside the point: his real offence had been to antagonise Warwick's daughters and their powerful husbands, a point demonstrated by his removal from all commissions, including commissions of the peace, at about the same time. Next, the sisters secured favourable verdicts from the inquisitions *post mortem* held on their father's lands: in all cases the juries ignored the 1349 entail and declared that the Berkeley inheritance in its entirety should descend to the daughters of the earl of Warwick as heirs general.

The situation looked bleak for James in the autumn of 1439. But as he had found after 1417, an inquisition's verdict meant nothing unless it could be enforced, and this time he was in possession of the disputed property. By February 1440 he still held all the properties he had entered the previous year, with the exception of a smattering of tenements in Wotton-under-Edge and Cowley. Quite how James was able to hold off his enemies for five months is a good question. Perhaps his overtures to Cardinal Beaufort had paid off. If so, this might explain why the Cardinal's nephew Edmund earl of Dorset and his wife Eleanor lost interest in the Berkeley dispute at around this time, but Lord and Lady Latimer were also drawing away from the engagement (Lord Latimer may already have been experiencing the mental health problems that would lead to the custody of his person and lands being granted to his brother, Salisbury, in 1451), leaving the Talbots to make the running.[26] Faced with an impasse, both sides agreed to go to arbitration. Among the arbiters, Berkeley's interests were represented by the duke of Gloucester, those of his opponents by Richard, duke of York, of whom Lord Talbot was a retainer. Proceedings dragged on for a year. Then, in February 1441, while Talbot was away in France, his brothers-in-law came to their own agreement with James.

The Talbots remained obdurate, however, and negotiations carried on sporadically for yet another year. They probably had no intention of settling on any terms that the Berkeleys would find acceptable. All the time, relations between the two families were on a knife edge: Smyth recounts how, when

Lord Talbot's son John, the future Lord Lisle, sent servants to serve a subpoena on Lord Berkeley at Wotton-under-Edge to appear in Chancery, James had them beaten up, and forced the bearer to eat the writ, both parchment and wax seal.[27] Finally, in 1442, Margaret Talbot, now countess of Shrewsbury, lost patience with the pretence of negotiation and decided to break the deadlock by resort to direct action. Her servants forced their way into the manors of Cowley, Simondshall and Wotton-under-Edge. Now she was ready to deal.

The new round of negotiations, with the Talbots very much calling the tune, continued for another six gruelling years, and it was not until April 1448 that James was forced to come to terms. Arbitration at Cirencester produced a settlement that was largely based on the 1425 agreement. This meant that the Talbots were allowed to keep the manors that Margaret had seized six years previously. While this fell short of handing the Talbots the ultimate prize, a hereditary interest in the entire disputed inheritance, it nonetheless promised to make permanent and legitimate what they had recently acquired by force. For James, it must have seemed as though the last nine years of struggle had been for nothing: he was, in effect, plunged back into the situation he had endured before Warwick's death. Presumably he gave some kind of acquiescence to the April settlement, but it was not long before he was trying to unravel it.

In July 1449 the arbiters required both parties to ratify their award by presenting a private bill before parliament. A settlement sanctioned by act of parliament would have been exceedingly difficult to renegotiate: it could only have been changed by another act, so James refused to be a party to this. With the Talbots enjoying favour at court and great influence in the county, James could do little more than hang on and wait for the next turn of Fortune's wheel. This came in the summer of 1450.

By now, the Lancastrian regime was in crisis. The French were sweeping through English territory, and Normandy was on the point of collapse. At home, lawlessness and corruption were rife. King Henry VI and his councillors were widely believed to have failed the two basic tests of kingship: they could neither defend the realm from foreign enemies, nor maintain order and stability within it. The summer of 1450 saw popular discontent reach its climax in the rebellion of Jack Cade, which spread across most of southern England. For a few days in July the rebels occupied London, while the king and his court fled to Kenilworth.

At this point, the court favour the Talbots could usually count on had been set at naught. Shrewsbury had been held hostage in France and would not return to England until December 1450, while his son, Lord Lisle, was away with the royal forces in the south east attempting to stem the tide of rebellion. Meanwhile, the death in June 1449 of Anne, granddaughter and heiress of Richard Beauchamp, earl of Warwick, and his second wife Isabel Despenser, had diverted the attention of Margaret and her two sisters and their husbands towards securing their share of the Beauchamp-Despenser inheritance, a much greater prize than the Berkeley claim, and one which was contested by Richard Neville, earl of Warwick, husband of Anne's aunt. Disputes within the Neville family over the Despenser inheritance also gave the Berkeleys an ally in the person of Edward, Lord Bergavenny, another of Salisbury's brothers, and a rival claimant to the earl of Warwick.[28] The Berkeleys did not let the opportunity slip by. William Berkeley and his men ransacked the Talbots' main Gloucestershire residence at Wotton-under-Edge. Countess Margaret would later allege, doubtless with some degree of exaggeration, that his men hacked through the main timbers, stripped out all the lead from the drains, conduits and sewers, and stole 4,000 marks worth of goods. The bill for the initial repair of all this damage she estimated at 1,600 marks. The Berkeleys' summer excursion to Wotton may have vented some of their frustration, but it had unwelcome – though predictable – consequences for their cause.

In September 1450 Lord Lisle procured a commission of *oyer et terminer*, headed by himself and the earl of Warwick, to investigate the attack on Wotton-under-Edge.[29] Such commissions had the power to hear cases, determine guilt, and punish the guilty to the full extent of the law. The commission posed a serious threat to the Berkeleys, since it effectively backed the Talbots' already considerable power with full judicial sanction. James, William and some of their associates were indicted, and took refuge in Berkeley Castle, which once again was placed under virtual siege.

Only a few miles separated the two armed camps of Berkeley Castle and Wotton-under-Edge: they are almost within sight of each other. Smyth speculated that Lord James's disputes with the Talbots 'produced the ill effects and destructions of a petty war' within Berkeley hundred. The feud's impact upon the borough of Berkeley was particularly severe:

> ...the burrowe Town of Berkeley, for her part, sawe the burning and prostration of many of her antient houses, as her old rent which till that time was – £22 by the year and upwards, and by those devastations brought down to eleven pounds and under, where it sticketh to this day, without recovery of her antient lustre or greatness.[30]

While there may have been other reasons for Berkeley's decline in a period when many towns were suffering contraction and economic difficulties, the depredations of warring factions must have made life difficult for those who had the misfortune to be tenants or neighbours of the Berkeley estate at this time.

Lady Isabel, meanwhile, was in London, supervising the Berkeleys' various legal proceedings. From here on 16 June 1451 she wrote a letter to her husband which gives a vivid impression of the desperate situation they faced:

> Right worshipfull and reverend lord and husband, I commend mee to you with all my whole hart, desyring alwayes to heare of your good wellfare, the which God maintayne and increase ever to your worship. And it please you to heare how I fare, Sir Squall and Squall; Thomas Roger and Jacket have asked surety of peace of mee, for their intent was to bring mee into the Tower, But I trust in God to morrow That I shall goe in bayle unto the next Terme, and soe to goe home And then to come againe; And Sur I trust to God and you will not treat with them, but keep your own in the most manlyest wise, yee shall have the land for ones and end; Bee well ware of Venables of Alderley, of Thom Mull and your false Counsell; keep well your place, The Earle of Shroesbury lyeth right nye unto you, and shapeth all the wyles that hee can to distrusse you and yours, for hee will not meddle with you openly no manner of wise, but it bee with great falsdome that hee can bring about or beguile you, or els that hee caused that yee have so fewe peopull about you, then will hee set on you, for hee saith hee will never come to the king againe till hee have done you an ill turn; Sur your matter speedeth and doth right well, save my daughter costeth great good; At the reverence of God send money or els I must lay my horse to pledge and come home on my feet: keep well all about you till I come home, and trete not without mee, And then all things shall be well with the grace of Almighty God, who have you in his keeping; written at London the wednesday next after whitsunday.
>
> Your wife the lady of Berkeley

Isabel did not have to walk home: James pawned a mass book, a silver chalice and chapel vestments to borrow twenty-two marks for her expenses.[31] The impression created by this letter is of a cool-headed, perhaps even courageous, eminently capable woman. Isabel appears to have been an astute judge of character: Richard Venables of Alderley, Gloucesterhire, was one of James's esquires, and in 1424/5 the recipient of a ten-mark annuity, but in 1451 he was also a Talbot retainer. Between 1420 and 1423 Thomas Mull had been a member of the Beauchamp household. He would soon play a part in the Talbots' attempts to ruin the Berkeleys.[32] The Talbots evidently had their agents even among Lord Berkeley's councillors. Isabel can countenance the threat of imprisonment in the Tower almost with insouciance, although we must remember that part of the purpose of this letter is to maintain her husband's morale. She is also capable of using humour to this end, if we are to interpret the address to James as 'Sir Squall and Squall' in this way; her comment about walking home also shows a light touch. Above all, however, what comes across is the full share that Isabel played in her family's affairs; indeed, her injunction to 'trete not without mee' could be interpreted as meaning that she was the dominant partner.

Three months later Berkeley Castle fell to the Talbots by subterfuge. The story of its fall could have come straight from the pen of Sir Walter Scott. Smyth reproduced two versions of events, one by Margaret Talbot, the other by William, then Lord Berkeley, as testimony in a Chancery case brought in 1466. Not surprisingly, they contradict each other at important points, and he gives his own version, offered, rather questionably, 'from him that partakes with neither party'. The accounts given by Smyth can be supplemented by allegations made in legal suits brought in 1475 by Lord William Berkeley and his brothers Maurice and Thomas, and John Wenlock, who in 1451 was a Talbot servant at Wotton-under-Edge.[33]

According to Margaret, one September night in 1451 William Berkeley sent twenty of his servants to the house of Richard Andrews, a tenant of the earl of Shrewsbury who lived ten miles away from the castle. Andrews was blind. The Berkeley men ransacked his house, and when they found little of value threatened to torture him with a red-hot branding iron, so that he told them where he had buried his treasure. Meanwhile, Viscount Lisle's men, having discovered that a company had ridden out of Berkeley Castle, had tracked them to the blind man's house. As the Berkeley men emerged with their ill-gotten gains they were surprised and overpowered by the Lisle party. One of the miscreants, Rhys Tewe, in fear of his life offered to get his captors inside Berkeley Castle, 'soe that they might take the residue of the said riotous misgoverned and endited people'. The Lisle men agreed to the plan and rode to the castle with Tewe. Once before the gates he called upon the watchman to open up. Suspecting nothing, the watchman collected the keys from Lord James and let them in. Once inside, they found not only James but also all four of his sons. This is certainly a colourful story, but one does wonder how the Talbot men were able, in the time it took the Berkeley men to ride ten miles, to detect the

Berkeley party at night, and then assemble a force strong enough to overwhelm the twenty armed men, before going on to seize control of the castle.

Lord William's version is rather more straightforward. There is no mention of Richard Andrews. Tewe was bribed by the Talbots to open the gates, and when the Talbots' men entered they found Lord Berkeley and his sons asleep in their beds and imprisoned them within their own castle for eleven weeks. According to Wenlock's testimony, in 1475 the Berkeleys were alleging that one of the younger sons of Lord James, Maurice, was taken at Wotton-under-Edge on the same night that his father and brothers were surprised in Berkeley Castle. In their own suits of that year the Berkeleys named four men who they claimed had been among their captors. Wenlock was one, and he was accompanied by a priest, John Howell, and by the Daunt brothers, Nicholas and John, the last of whom played an important part at Nibley Green.[34]

There is broad agreement on what happened next, but not over the motives and behaviour of those involved. The accounts given by Smyth can also be filled out by testimony given in King's Bench.[35] The earl of Shrewsbury himself was probably absent during the following proceedings, and so it was Margaret who took the initiative after the capture of the Berkeleys. On 4 October the Berkeleys were brought before an *oyer et terminer* commission at Chipping Campden, where they were condemned for their attack on Wotton-under-Edge and ordered to pay the Talbots £1,000 in cash, and make other compensation, while Berkeley Castle was to be granted to the Talbots as surety for payment. James was bound to Lisle in 700 marks, and his eldest son William was to become Lisle's retainer, which meant that he had to promise to serve Lisle, giving him loyalty before all others apart from the king and his cousin John, duke of Norfolk (the following year his two brothers, Thomas and William, were indented to serve with the earl of Shrewsbury in France). The Talbots' right to Wotton-under-Edge was confirmed, and the Berkeleys were ordered to pledge a further £10,000 as a recognisance to bind them to observe these arrangements. After this hearing Margaret forced them to put their seals to twelve deeds which granted away properties and leased Berkeley Castle to the countess for two years. Among the five named witnesses to one of these deeds was the sheriff of Gloucestershire, Henry Clifford, a Talbot councillor who used his office to aid Margaret's persecution of the Berkeleys; John Guise and Robert Stanshaw, both Talbot retainers; and Thomas Mull, the man against whom Lady Isabel had warned her husband four months earlier.[36]

The following month the hapless Berkeleys were taken down to Bristol where, at a mayor's court held – rather irregularly – at the house of the grey friars, they were bound over to keep the peace and pledged to find an additional £12,204 in compensation and surety. In 1466 Lord William represented these concessions for what they surely were, exactions made under extreme duress; Margaret, on the other hand, tried to convince the court that the Berkeleys, suddenly realising how dreadfully they had behaved, followed the advice given by their council learned that it was time to make amends. These insults and injuries were insufficient vengeance for Margaret. Between December 1451 and October 1452 she made three attempts to challenge the 1349 entail before the commissioners of *oyer et terminer*. Despite the Talbots' power and influence, and – Smyth is in no doubt – her ruthless manipulation of juries, she failed. She did, however, manage to have all Lord Berkeley's Gloucestershire and Somerset manors confiscated to satisfy the terms of the £10,000 recognisance.

The various bonds and recognisances enforced upon the Berkeleys would not be nullified for over a quarter of a century. Extricating himself from them would usher in the last and most bizarre phase of William, Lord Berkeley's career. For now, the Berkeleys had been forced to acquiesce in what appeared to be the final ruination of their fortunes. But this was not the worst to befall Lord James in the terrible twelve months after the fall of Berkeley Castle.

The second of Margaret Talbot's attempts to challenge the Berkeley titles took place at Gloucester in 1452. According to a Chancery suit brought by Lord William Berkeley in 1464/5, his mother appeared before the *oyer et terminer* commissioners to plead her husband's case. Isabel was seized and imprisoned in Gloucester Castle, where she died soon after. William went on to claim that on the night of her imprisonment a man named Lacon was murdered by his servant. Before his execution the servant confessed that 'hee was tempted to murder his master for his untrue dealing in the said enquest'. This story might sound like a fiction contrived by William or his lawyers to add weight to his plea, but there was a Lacon among the Talbot retainers, Richard the younger, of Willey in Shropshire: the single record we have of a fee being paid to him occurs in 1452.[37] Smyth certainly believed that Isabel's death was murder, and portrayed the killing of Thomas, Lord Lisle at Nibley Green as William Berkeley's revenge for this crime. Looked at objectively, however, this assumption might appear rash. Quite simply, the Talbots did not have enough to gain from Isabel's murder to make it a sensible risk to take. They had already crushed her family to the point where they offered no real threat for the foreseeable future, and the cold-blooded murder of a baroness and daughter of the ducal house of Norfolk would be bound to bring retribution, even for the earl and countess of Shrewsbury. Medieval prisons were not healthy places, and Isabel might simply have been one among the many who succumbed to disease as the result of their incarceration. The actual manner of her death is in one respect beside the point. The news of his wife's death must have been a devastating blow to Lord James, and in the circumstances one can well imagine how he and his sons would immediately assume that she had been murdered. What they thought had happened is the important point, and if they thought that she had been murdered, then Isabel's death had the potential to turn a property dispute into a blood feud.

More tragedy came in the following year. On 17 July 1453, at Castillon, the earl of Shrewsbury rashly charged a heavily fortified French position. He was hit in the leg by a cannon ball and then hacked to death, as were his companions in arms. Among the dead was James, second son of Lord Berkeley, who had been forced to serve in the Talbot retinue as part of the order made the previous year. His younger brother Thomas, not yet nineteen, fought with him for the same reason, and was captured. His ransom would be an almost unbearable burden upon his family's already impoverished estate. Even so, Castillon was a greater tragedy for Margaret Talbot, for slain on the same battlefield as her husband was their son, John, Lord Lisle.

The deaths of these two John Talbots, father and son, changed everything. The second earl of Shrewsbury, another John, was the son of the previous earl by his first marriage. Margaret had tried and failed to disinherit the children of her predecessor, and there was now deep enmity between Earl John and his step-mother. He did not share Margaret's obsession with the Berkeley inheritance. After his succession, hostilities between Berkeley and Talbot all but ceased and in July 1457 the two families made a genuine peace. The pact was sealed by a remarkable marriage. At the age of sixty-three James, Lord Berkeley, took to wife Joan, sister of the second earl of Shrewsbury. The marriage settlement was also, in effect, an indenture of retainer, by which Shrewsbury promised to be Berkeley's good lord, who would support him in all his quarrels. That until recently Berkeley's quarrels had been largely with the family of his new brother-in-law would have been an irony not lost on the happy couple. Nor would the implications have been lost on Margaret Talbot: in the words of Smyth, by this marriage Berkeley 'not only gave strength to his own affaires, but hee weakened the power of the adverse party'.[38]

Not everyone in the Berkeley camp was happy with the Talbot marriage.[39] Smyth believed that Sir William, son and heir of Lord James, regarded his new step-mother as a manipulator, taking advantage of her husband's weaknesses 'by beating upon ye weake pulse of her husbands old age'. The tension

17. James (d. 1453), with his father, James, Lord Berkeley (d. 1463) behind him. In the background can be seen Lord Henry (d. 1613), and his wife Katherine: the Berkeley Mortuary Chapel, St Mary's, Berkeley.

between father and son may have predated the marriage. That it afterwards continued, and probably intensified, is demonstrated by the text of an agreement drawn up between the two in August 1460. From the terms of this document it would seem that James was actually afraid of his eldest son. Sir William agreed not to molest his father's servants, nor to maintain his father's enemies. He undertook not to enter the lordship of Berkeley accompanied by more than ten persons without his father's permission, to give his father half a day's notice of his coming, and not to stay longer than a week. He also promised not to enfeoff or alienate the manor of Portbury or any part of it. Portbury was Sir William's main place of residence, and its management had been a bone of contention six years earlier, when William had leased it to the earl of Wiltshire despite having promised his father that he would not do so. Portbury, James believed, had been the first land his ancestors had ever purchased in England, and so he disapproved of any arrangement that might result in its loss to the family.

On 4 March 1461 England had a new king. Edward, son of Richard, duke of York, had toppled Henry VI and taken the throne as Edward IV. One of his most powerful supporters was Richard, earl of Warwick. The new regime was bad news for Margaret Talbot and her sisters, for Warwick did not scruple to use his new-found ascendancy against his rival claimants to the Beauchamp-Despenser inheritance.[40] Politically isolated, Margaret came to terms with the Berkeleys in October 1463.

Sir William was probably unhappy with the settlement made between his father and the countess of Shrewsbury, by which they agreed to be satisfied with the estates they then held and not to pursue any more legal suits. This meant that the Berkeleys' old enemy still held the entailed manors of Wotton-under-Edge, Cowley and Simondshall, together with Sages and Newlyes, but James, at least, had evidently given up hope of ever getting these back. He was now sixty-nine years old and exhausted by a lifetime of struggle.

William succeeded to this diminished inheritance on his father's death in November 1463.[41] From the start, he was determined to recover the disputed manors. Smyth describes Lord William and 'malitious Margaret Countess of Shrewsbury', as 'two merciless natures not unevenly encountringe... whose mutuall hatreds each to other, ended not before their breaths', and Margaret proved herself a worthy match for the new Lord Berkeley. Suit and counter suit once more flew around the law courts, reciting the litany of wrongs each side had perpetrated on the other over the many years of the dispute. There were also fresh allegations, such as that contained in a Chancery suit brought by William in 1466/7. In this he claimed that Margaret had hired a criminal called Chamberlain, who had taken refuge in the sanctuary next to Westminster Abbey, to murder William as he left London; the plot was thwarted when Thomas Oldbury, 'a well disposed man' persuaded the would-be assassin to reveal all to William. Chamberlain then arranged for some of Berkeley's servants to be hidden within earshot as one of Margaret's men exhorted Chamberlain to commit the deed. In reply, Margaret claimed that William had taken sanctuary at Westminster to avoid the writs of outlawry directed against him as a result of Margaret's suits. Chamberlain had offered only to lure William out of sanctuary so that these writs could be served. Chamberlain then – in 1464/5 – spread the rumour that Margaret had hired him as an assassin, but after investigating these claims the abbot of Westminster, who had authority over the inhabitants of the sanctuary,

> decreed him to bee had to an open place in the sanctuary of punishment and reproofe, And made him to bee arayed in papires painted with signes of untroth, sedition, and doublenesse, And was made to goe before the procession in that aray, and afterwards soe set in the stocks, that the people might behold him.

Where the truth lies in these stories it is now impossible to say, but William might well have been in the Westminster sanctuary, sheltering from Margaret's writs after his father's death, before fleeing to Berkeley Castle. As a liberty, Berkeley also gave him some immunity from legal process. He did not find reclaiming his ancestral home an easy business. Elsewhere in the same Chancery case William accuses Margaret of having tried to suborn Thomas Holt, keeper of Berkeley Castle, to deny access to him after his father's death. This was a claim that Margaret did not deny. Had she been successful, Berkeley, having fled from sanctuary in London, would have found the gates of his own castle barred against him, and would thereby have been danger-ously exposed to the process of law. As it is, it seems that entrance to Berkeley Castle was indeed denied him for a while after his return from London, so that he had to force his way in, although we can only speculate if it was Margaret's men or his father's old retainers who kept him out.[42]

Margaret Talbot, Countess of Shrewsbury, died in June 1467. At her death William, Lord Berkeley, had possession of Berkeley Castle, but the five disputed manors of Wotton, Cowley, Simondshall, Sages and Newleyes remained in Talbot hands and, along with other properties in Gloucestershire and in as many as nine other counties, were inherited by Margaret's grandson and heir, the nineteen-year-old Thomas, Viscount Lisle.[43] Lisle's parents pre-deceased his grandmother, and the wardship and custody of the lands of the under-age Thomas were acquired by William, Lord Herbert, soon to be created earl of Pembroke, who was Edward IV's most powerful lieutenant in Wales. As part of Herbert's policy of extending his power through family alliances he married Lisle to Margaret, one of his daughters. The marriage brought Lisle within the extended royal family, since Herbert's son and heir was married to a sister of Elizabeth Woodville, Edward IV's new queen.[44] Herbert's influence came to Thomas relatively late in his short life. After the death of his father and grandfather in 1453, it was probably his grandmother, the formidable Margaret, who had the greatest part in forming his opinions. If so, there can be little doubt that he was inculcated with a deep hostility towards the Berkeleys.[45] Also, on attaining his majority in July 1469, he may have felt that he had to prove himself worthy to be the grandson of the great earl of Shrewsbury. William, Lord Berkeley and Thomas, Viscount Lisle had inherited both the dispute and their predecessors' single-mindedness in pursuit of it. The stage was set for Nibley Green.

2

THE BATTLE

Smyth recounts how in January 1470 Lisle sought to gain possession of Berkeley Castle by a subterfuge similar to that employed successfully by his grandmother nineteen years earlier.[1] Through one of his tenants, Robert Vele, described by Smyth as his 'Ingineer', Lisle was able to bribe Thomas Holt, who was by then Berkeley's keeper of Whitcliff Park, and may still have been keeper of Berkeley Castle. Holt's loyalties must surely have been suspect since at least 1466/7, when he was named in Lord Berkeley's Chancery bill as having been in receipt of letters from Margaret. That he should have remained in Berkeley's service demands some explanation. Berkeley would later claim, after Holt's final treachery, that he, 'of his own free will undesired of mee, before worshipful and sufficient witnes, was sworn on a masse booke, that hee never should bee a gainst mee in noe matter that I had a doe'.

Smyth's materials for his account of the plot of January 1470 are drawn from a single roll in the Berkeley muniment room, produced at some time soon after the events of 1470.[2] None of the material contained in the roll is extant in other, independent sources, so we have to treat it with some caution. The roll begins with the text of a letter to Maurice King, porter of Berkeley Castle, from 'your sworn brother', Thomas Holt. In this letter Holt reminds King of their long-standing friendship and,

> spetially for the great truth and faithful love that I found in you at the appointment between the lord Berkeley that now is, and us; and by the token that when Mr Thomas [a chaplain, according to Smyth's marginal note] had gave up the matter and failed us, that ye and I yede [went] into the Chapple out of the great chamber, And there I found you true, as you ever have bene hyderto.

Does this obscure episode relate to the accusations made in 1466/7? Had it been Thomas who revealed all to Lord Berkeley, perhaps in the Great

Chamber, and on witnessing this King and Holt hurried into the nearby chapel to hatch a plan to save themselves – a plan which may have involved Holt's oath-taking? Holt may have persuaded Lord Berkeley that he had been no more than the passive recipient of Margaret's letters – although his failure to reveal their existence to his master might be thought sufficient of itself to warrant his dismissal – but this letter would seem to prove that his intentions had been more sinister. The letter, like that of Isabel to Lord James in 1451, suggests that the Berkeley household was a place of whispered plots and doubtful loyalties, infiltrated by Talbot agents.

Turning back to the text of the letter: Holt then requests that King give 'very faythfull credence unto Mr Robert Vele', as a gentleman whose trust-worthiness was attested both by Holt himself and by 'my lord': presumably this is Viscount Lisle, not Lord Berkeley! King and Vele were to discuss 'what night ye may in hasty time speke with mee'.

Immediately below the text of this letter is a short note, again from Holt to King, assuring him that '...for your matter, it is spede, your patent is spede of five markes and Wotton parke, with all that belongeth theirto, and your obligac[i]on also...'. The text of the obligation and patent follow. The obligation is dated 26 January 1470; it is a guarantee that if King does not receive a patent, or formal grant, of the custody of Wotton Park, with its accompanying fees and wages, together with a lifetime annuity of five marks, before 2 February, then by this day Robert Vele will pay King £100. The obligation makes clear that the grant of Wotton Park and the annuity is to be King's reward for helping to deliver Berkeley Castle into the hands of Viscount Lisle. Vele's obligation to King indicates that the conspirators assumed that the castle would be delivered within the week. Smyth tells us that Lisle was so delighted with Vele's plan that he gave to his brother, William Vele, the stewardship of the manor of Wotton and the keepership of Michaelwood Chase. However, Lisle's delight was short-lived. As Smyth relates, 'This plot thus contrived and brought to ripeness was soon after revealed to this lord Will[ia]m, And, as I take it, by Maurice Kinge himselfe...'. When it came to the crunch, Wotton Park and five marks a year were insufficient, it seems, to persuade King to treachery. Things may not have been entirely as they were represented, however. In 1472 a Maurice King would figure as one of the feoffees to Berkeley Castle and the other disputed properties. If this was the same man, then Berkeley was extraordinarily forgiving, or perhaps King had been acting as a double agent and *agent provocateur* all the time.[3] Once more compromised, Holt this time made no attempt to talk himself out of his predicament, and instead sought refuge with Lisle. According to Smyth, the thwarted Lisle 'then begins to unmask himself, & openly to act his ill cogitations'.

On the same roll that contains the texts of the January plot, and following on immediately after them, are what purport to be the texts of two letters (see the Appendix), one a challenge, sent from Viscount Lisle to Lord Berkeley on 19 March 1470, the other Berkeley's reply, sent the same day. Lisle's letter challenges Berkeley to single combat or, failing that, to battle with their respective forces. Berkeley's letter of reply rejects single combat, but demands battle the following day – 20 March – at Nibley Green. The original letters – if they ever existed – have not survived. The texts on the roll appear to have been produced all at the same time, in a hand typical of the last third of the fifteenth century. These two letters must be considered at some length. As well as appearing to supply vital information on the events leading up to the battle, they also provide a unique insight into the motivations and mental world of their composers, even if these were not Viscount Lisle and Lord Berkeley. As with the materials concerning the January plot, there is the possibility – in fact quite a strong possibility in this case – that the texts are not entirely what they represent themselves to be.[4]

The challenge and response are texts redolent of the spirit of later medieval chivalry. The battle of Nibley Green cannot properly be understood without entering into the mental world of the later medieval chivalric knight. Lisle's challenge and Berkeley's response open a door into that world. The Lisle letter begins with the address, 'William, called lord Berkeley', thereby refusing to acknowledge the legitimacy of his title. For his part, Berkeley opens his response with an address that attempts to cast a slur on Viscount Lisle's superior title: 'Thomas Talbot, otherwise called viscont Lisle, not longe continued in that name but a new found thing brought out of Strange Contryes...'. Berkeley's family, of course, had enjoyed noble status for centuries: but they were mere barons. Lisle was a viscount, and so outranked Baron Berkeley. On the other hand, Lord Berkeley could console himself, and seek to irritate Viscount Lisle, by remembering that the rank of viscount had only existed in the English realm since 1385; what is more, it had been a foreign introduction, and a French one at that![5] Ironically, eleven years later Lord Berkeley's qualms about the novelty of the title would not prevent him from accepting it, to become Viscount Berkeley; and not content with this, he would end his life as a marquis, a title equally 'foreign' and newfangled.[6]

The ridiculing of Lisle's title may have been part of a wider slur upon what in a later age might have been called his patriotism. In his challenge, Lisle tells Berkeley that he would meet him,

18. The Great Hall, Berkeley Castle.

with English men of my one nation and neighbors, whereas ye by suttle craft have blowin about in divers places of England, That I should intend to bring in Welshmen for to destroy and hurt my one nation and Cuntry;

Berkeley, it seems, had been using Lisle's family connections to stoke up English xenophobia, or more precisely, Cymro-phobia, against him. Berkeley is here using Lisle's marriage to Margaret, daughter of William Herbert, earl of Pembroke, to suggest that his loyalties lay more with his wife's compatriots than with his own. Herbert was executed in July 1469 after his defeat at the battle of Edgecote on the orders of the earl of Warwick. At that battle, English and Welsh fought against each other, but they did so as adherents of English lords and English kings: it had been almost sixty years since the Welsh, under Owain Glyn Dŵr, had last raised their swords as rebels – or freedom fighters – against the King of England.[7] The revolt left a grim legacy of ethnic hatred and discrimination, but by the 1460s much of that bitterness had faded. The penal statutes that had established a virtual apartheid between Welsh and English had last been issued in 1447, and were now habitually ignored. Welshmen were beginning to build careers in England, and William Herbert himself had been one of Edward IV's most trusted lieutenants.[8] Incidentally, it would be wrong to assume from Herbert's English-sounding name that he was a thoroughly Anglicised, *soi-disant* Celt. William, the son of William ap Thomas and Gwladys, daughter of Dafydd Gam (a hero of Agincourt), was a noted patron of bards and as much at home in Welsh culture as in English.[9] Judging by Lisle's sensitivity about his in-laws, however, not every Englishman shared Edward IV's acceptance of the Welsh, and it would seem that Berkeley had been spreading rumours that his opponent intended to ravage Gloucestershire with these unruly foreigners. Such stories might have found a ready reception among those whose parents had suffered the depredations of unruly Beauchamp followers brought from across the Severn in the 1420s.[10]

Having dealt with this slur on his Englishness, Lisle then requires Berkeley, since he will not come to Wotton, 'of knighthood and of manhood to appoynt a day to meet me half way'. Lisle invokes two ideals, 'knighthood' and 'manhood', which he expects – quite correctly, if we are to accept these documents as genuine – to have sufficient power to compel Berkeley to fight him. What did these words mean in the fifteenth century?

Beginning with knighthood, and to take the question at its most literal, 'knight' is derived from the Old English word *cniht*, meaning, simply, warrior. During the earlier Middle Ages the word was used to describe an armoured, mounted warrior of gentle birth, and such men dominated European battle-fields, but by 1470 the knight was no longer the military phenomenon he had once been. English armies rarely fought on horseback, and battles were more likely to be decided by masses of yeomen archers than by iron-clad aristocrats. Certainly, at a private battle such as Nibley Green, with most of the participants drawn from the opposing lords' tenantry, the well-equipped, armoured men-at-arms would have been in the minority. With the end of the Hundred Years' War in 1453, the knightly class spent most of its time supervising its estates, sitting on commissions, or wheeling and dealing in the corridors of power; martial or equestrian adventures were limited to hunting, the occasional squabble with neighbours or the rare participation in tournaments. The battles of the Wars of the Roses would have engaged relatively few of the gentry, and were hardly the stuff of chivalric romance. In one sense, fifteenth-century knighthood had already become what it is today: a title granted by the monarch in recognition of service, social status, economic power and political influence; but only in one sense, for knighthood as an ideal was still largely what it had been in the golden age of chivalry.

Browsing the libraries of the gentry and nobility, one would expect to find, alongside the standard aids to devotion and legal treatises, works of chivalric literature: manuals, setting out exempla of knightly conduct, and tales of famous knights, both real and imagined. Looking at the tapestries and painted cloths adorning their walls, one might see depicted paragons of chivalry down the ages: Achilles, Hercules, Arthur, Richard the Lionheart and even the English heroes of the Hundred Years' War – perhaps, even, Lord Lisle's own grandfather, the 'English Achilles'. Fifteenth-century noblemen did think of themselves as occupying the same universe as an Arthurian hero, and acted accordingly. Lisle's challenge and Berkeley's response are the products of this culture. Even if their motivations were vendetta and greed, and the resultant battle a sordid skirmish in a muddy field in Gloucestershire, they portrayed themselves as fighting to defend name and honour, through the exercise of their knightly prowess. Nor is there any reason to think that they did not sincerely believe their own publicity.

Perhaps it is difficult for us to come to terms with the apparent contradiction between chivalric ideals and self-seeking violence, because our concept of what chivalry was – seen, inescapably, through the rosy lens of Tennyson – is very different from what it was actually held to be in the later Middle Ages. Central to the chivalric code was the glorification of violence, or prowess. His prowess, encompassing physical strength, skill at arms, and courage, is what Lisle is challenging Berkeley to prove. Prowess was not, necessarily, what we might recognise as a moral or ethical virtue.[11] The right to exercise violence was one of the attributes of the 'gentle' classes, as it was, in a domestic setting, of an adult male of any rank. The right of the gentry and nobility to use violence to defend their community, either from outside aggression or from criminals, was an extension of the right of all men to use violence to keep order among their inferiors. Male heads of household were widely agreed – at least by other men – to have the right to beat children, servants and wives, provided this did not cause permanent injury. Those men without the will or ability to impose order within their sphere of influence were derided as effeminate. Hence, masculinity – Lisle's 'manhood' – was inextricably linked with prowess. If Berkeley had not met Lisle's challenge with force of arms, both his social and sexual status would have been impugned.

To prove his knighthood, to demonstrate his manhood, and to rescue his honour, Berkeley was challenged to a duel, 'to try between God and our two hands, all our quarrell and title of right'. This is not to be confused with either trial by combat, or the judicial duel.[12] Trial by combat, the notion that guilt or innocence could be determined through divine intervention in a straight fight between plaintiff and defendant, or their representatives, was rarely employed by the fifteenth century. The judicial duel was more common, however. Writing under Henry VI, Nicholas Upton, an authority on matters martial and chivalric, was of the opinion that the judicial duel, if authorised by a legitimate authority, 'is for honour' and 'is done principally to prove [the participants'] strength and manhood'. The judicial duel was a formal procedure, usually resorted to in situations of martial law, particularly where the protagonists came from opposing sides in the conflict and so where matters of honour could not easily be tried before a court. The most famous example in English history is the projected combat between Henry Bolingbroke and Thomas Mowbray, dramatised in Shakespeare's *Richard II*. While this did not occur during wartime, it did involve a matter of honour which, through lack of evidence, could not otherwise be resolved. Canon law looked askance at the whole business, but lay opinion tended to allow the judicial duel as legitimate, provided that the protagonists could demonstrate that their honour was at stake, that there was insufficient evidence for the case to be tried before judge and jury, and that both parties were of sufficient rank. These could be difficult criteria to meet, and many challenges ended bloodlessly and indecisively, like that between Bolingbroke and Mowbray. The judicial duel was not, in the fifteenth century, a half-forgotten anachronism. The last example in England would take place at Westminster in 1571.

19. Single combat.

What Lisle had in mind, however, did not meet the criteria of judicial duel. There is no suggestion in his challenge that all other legal processes had been exhausted – a point made in Berkeley's response – nor that any higher authority would be asked to adjudicate. Rather, this is a straightforward private duel, of the sort that would continue to be fought by European gentlemen up to the twentieth century. Lisle offers an interesting rationale for his proposal. The two lords are '...to try between God and our two hands, all our quarrell and title of right...'. The *casus belli* itself is a disputed claim to property, not a matter of honour. The injury to either protagonist's honour would derive from his refusal to accept the challenge, not from the original cause of the dispute. That refusal, however, would have been a grievous thing. The outcome would not only be decided by God's will, for individual prowess would also play its part: might is, to some extent, right. This doubtless seemed an attractive proposition to a man of twenty-three facing an opponent almost twice his age.

Whatever calculation Lisle may have made about the likely outcome of a one-to-one duel, he proposed single combat ostensibly 'to eschew the shedding of Christian menns bloud...'. Challenges to single combat as a means of avoiding unnecessary bloodshed were part of the common rhetoric of European aristocrats. Emperor Charles V twice challenged Francis I of France to such a combat, but they never met sword to sword: this was the usual – perhaps inevitable – outcome. The offer having been made, the opponent who had declined it could then be portrayed as one who cared not for the unnecessary bloodshed his refusal would bring about. And so it was in March 1470. Berkeley's confident reply is quite correct: 'thou wottest right well there is noe such determinac[i]on of land in this Relme used'. He went on to add:

> And if it were soe That this matter might bee determined by thy honds and myne, the king our Soveraigne lord and his laws not offended, thou shouldst not so longe desire but I would assoone answere thee, in every poynt that belongeth to a knight...

So, battle it was to be, with Berkeley boasting that, 'I will thou understand, that I will not bring the tenth part that I can make.' Here, to modern eyes, there seems to be the most staggering logical disjuncture: Berkeley refuses single combat because it is illegal, so instead proposes a full-scale battle between their retainers! Berkeley makes no attempt to square this particular circle, but he does try to absolve himself of responsibility for the bloodshed that is likely to result:

for thou art, God I take to record, in a false quarrell, and I in a true defence and title... And remember, thy self and thy false Counsell have refused to abide the rule of the grete lordis of this lond, which by my will should have determyned this matter by thy evidence and mine,[13] And therefore I vouch God to record and all the company of heaven, That this fact and the scheddinge of Christen mens bloud which shall be atwixt us two and our fellowshipps, if any hap to bee, doth grow of thy quaryll, and not of mee, but in my defence, and in eschewing of reproche, and only through thy malitious and mischevouse purpose and of thy false Counsell, and of thy own simple discretion.

Such formal challenges to combat are rare in fifteenth-century England, but not unique.[14] In 1455, in the midst of a bitter conflict over land and status in Devon, William Lord Bonville issued a written challenge to combat to Thomas Courtenay, earl of Devon. As with Lisle and Berkeley, the two men were to meet, with their followers, at a time and place appointed, but there is an important difference. Repeatedly, Bonville appeals to the good of the common weal in his challenge. The violent excesses of the earl and his men have brought fear and confusion to the people of Devon, and in the absence of effective royal authority Bonville is willing to risk life and limb as their champion:

Promittyng the as I am the kinges trewe liegeman & knighte that I shall in my diffence vppon the premisses as for the commune wele of all the kynges trew liege people and namely for the dwelleres of this shire ful redy to rencontre the & topteyne or dye.

Devon is being portrayed as the ogre or dragon, from whom Bonville, the knight in shining armour, has to deliver his people. Neither Lisle nor Berkeley make any such claims. Beyond their avowed desires to avoid the unnecessary shedding of blood in their quarrel, the sole hint of altruism comes from Berkeley's bitter recrimination against his turncoat servant Holt:

And as for the false mischevous Holt, what his rule hath be to the destruction of the kings lege pepull in my lordship of Berkeley, aswell to the hurt of their bodyes, as the losse of their goods, against Godys lawe, consciens, and all reason, it is openly known...

But even here, the inhabitants of the lordship are little more than an extension of Berkeley's own affronted persona.

Berkeley's diatribe links Holt with another of Lisle's 'false untrue Counsell': Hugh Mull. He is accused of being 'attaynt of falseness and rasinge of the kings records'. Falsifying or obliterating the records of royal government was a felony, and so this was a serious accusation. Had he actually been attainted, Mull's property would have been confiscated, and his heirs deprived of their inheritance. He was probably related to Thomas Mull, a witness to the Berkeleys' forced surrender of disputed property in 1451, and against whom Lady Isabel had warned this Lord Berkeley's father.[15]

Lisle's challenge and Berkeley's acceptance were dated the same day, 19 March. Berkeley appointed the time and place of battle: they were to meet the following morning, at eight, at Nibley Green, midway between their two strongholds of Berkeley and Wotton-under-Edge. This gave them less than twenty-four hours in which to gather their forces and march to Nibley Green. Smyth believed that Berkeley may have had about a thousand men at Nibley Green, and that Lisle's force was smaller. Chroniclers are notoriously prone to inflating the numbers involved in battles, but given the size of Berkeley's holdings, it is conceivable that he could have raised such a number, given time.

Two cases brought before the court of King's Bench after the battle give valuable evidence for the composition of the two armies. They also raise interesting questions about the authenticity of the challenge and response texts as documents produced on the day before Nibley Green. One of the two King's Bench suits was begun by Margaret Viscountess Lisle in Trinity Term (June/July) 1471 and is summarised by Smyth; the other, undiscovered by Smyth, was brought in Hilary Term (January/February) 1471 by Agnes Lewis, who claimed that her husband, John Lewis, had been killed at Nibley Green.[16] Both widows named the alleged murderers and their associates. From the King's Bench evidence we have the names of eighteen men alleged to have been present, including Lisle and the Berkeley brothers Maurice and Thomas. Smyth writes of how,

> Maurice out of brotherly love to him [William, Lord Berkeley] and his honor, upon ye short warning of one night at most, stole from his young wife and tender son... and met him with a fair band of men, Mr Hilpe, and others, suddainly raised from Thornbury, where hee then dwelt, early the next morning near Nibley green.[17]

The 'Mr Hilpe' in question was probably Richard Hylpe, named in Margaret Talbot's plea as a cordwainer late of Paganhill, near Stroud, which is, like Thornbury, about ten miles from Berkeley. His fellow defendant, John Beley, a

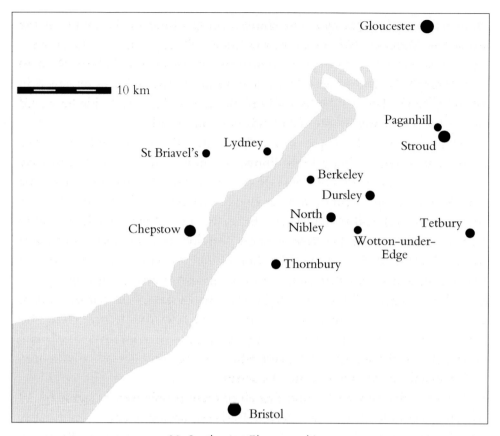

20. South-west Gloucestershire.

husbandman, was also from Paganhill. Others named by Margaret were: John Bendall, a yeoman from Berkeley; John Sawnders, a cook from Gloucester; John Body, a Bristol painter; and James Hyett, constable of the castle of St Briavel's in the Forest of Dean, and the man Leland accused of Lisle's murder. James Hyett was an esquire of Newland and Lydney in the Forest of Dean, and had been holding land in the area since at least 1444. His wife Alice and brother Robert appear with him in deeds, and he was dead by March 1484, having been predeceased by his eldest son Roger, leaving as his heir his younger son Thomas, of Lydney, a gentleman. In 1464 and 1473 he was described in deeds simply as 'constable', suggesting some of the local renown that his position gave him.[18]

There is other evidence that implicates likely participants in the battle. Lord Berkeley later granted an annuity of four marks to John Cassey esquire for his good service at the battle. Cassey was sheriff of Gloucestershire in 1469 and 1470, so it is possible that he used his position to raise men on Berkeley's behalf. On 15 May 1470 Lord Berkely granted a life annuity to Richard

Beauchamp of Powick, Worcestershire, to be paid out of the profits of the manor of Wotton.[19] The timing of this grant, and the source of the annuity, strongly suggests that this was in return for his support at Nibley: Richard Beauchamp now had a vested interest in ensuring that Wotton remained in Berkeley hands. He was the son of Lord Beauchamp, to which title he would succeed in 1475, and he also held lands in Gloucestershire.[20]

Finally, there is the copy of a judgement, still in the Berkeley Castle muniment room, made by John Shipward senior, mayor of Bristol, in May 1470.[21] Mayor Shipward concluded that, contrary to the slander put about by evil-disposed people, two prominent Bristol merchants, John Shipward junior (the mayor's son), and Philip Mede – father-in-law of Lord Berkeley's brother Maurice – did not 'send certayn persoones forcibly arrayd in manner of warre to the Lord Berkeley azeynst the Lord Lisle'. Smyth, however, was not convinced, and claims that family documents in his possession prove that a Bristol contingent did in fact fight for the Berkeleys at Nibley Green. Berkeley's greater resources and influence in the area may be reflected by his apparent ability to call upon contingents under the command of leading Bristolians, of the sheriff of Gloucestershire, of the constable of a royal castle, and, probably, of the future Lord Beauchamp.

Assuming that this was so, and that all of these people were at home on 19 March when Lisle's letter was received, Berkeley, having discussed Lisle's letter with his council, would then have had to despatch his messengers to Paganhill, Stroud, Thornbury, Gloucester, Bristol and across the River Severn to the Forest of Dean, to raise his troops in time to muster at Nibley Green by early the next morning. This would simply not have been possible without advance notice days before the receipt of Lisle's letter. The obvious conclusion is that Berkeley was expecting some sort of attack after the discovery of Lisle's plot to betray the castle, and had either warned his affinity to be ready at a moment's notice, or had brought some of them to stay at Berkeley Castle. Even had he adopted the former course of action, getting his forces together in one place at such short notice would have been very difficult. The probability, then, is that Berkeley Castle and its environs was already accommodating a sizeable proportion of the men that would fight for Lord Berkeley at Nibley Green. Such a state of readiness could not be sustained for very long (it had been seven weeks since the discovery of the plot), and so it is likely that Berkeley had in some way provoked Lord Lisle into this action, knowing that he was better prepared than his adversary. The fact that he gave Lisle only until the following morning to raise his forces might suggest this. While Lisle had some Gloucestershire manors, his main strength probably lay outside the county. His known

21. Bristol's sheriff and two sergeants, from from *The Mayor of Bristol's Kalendar*, 1479/80.

supporters at Nibley Green came from a very restricted area encompassing Wotton, Dursley, Stroud and Tetbury. The longer Berkeley waited, the more time Lisle had to bring in reinforcements from further afield: Berkeley's men, on the other hand, are likely to have been numerous, ready and waiting.

That Berkeley may somehow have manipulated Lisle into issuing his challenge gives rise to a further, altogether more tentative speculation. Given that the earliest extant texts of the documents relating to the plot of January 1470 and the challenge and response are all found as copies on the same roll, it might be suggested that these are, in whole or in part, forgeries, designed to clear Berkeley from the accusation that he provoked Lisle into a fatal trap. There seems little doubt that the copying of these documents was done with the intention of demonstrating that Berkeley was more sinned against than sinning. As such, the likelihood is that they were made in 1471–72, when Berkeley was prosecuted in King's Bench by Viscountess Lisle. But there is quite a jump from this to the suggestion of forgery. On the other hand, it is perhaps a little surprising that on receipt of Lisle's challenge on 19 March, and having decided to meet him the next day, Berkeley – or one of his counsel-

1 and 2. Nibley House, an eighteenth-century view. The ranges in the stable courtyard may preserve part of John Smyth's house.

3. Nibley House today is a farm and bed and breakfast hotel.

4. St Martin's Church, North Nibley, the burial place of John Smyth.

5. The east end of Bristol Cathedral, originally part of St Augustine's Abbey.

6. Berkeley Castle gatehouse.

8. The former St Mary's Chapel, Berkeley Castle.

Opposite 7. The Lord Mayor's Chapel, Bristol, originally part of St Mark's Hospital, founded by a branch of the fitz Harding family.

9. Gallery, formerly in St Mary's Chapel, Berkeley Castle.

10. Nibley Green from Shankley Hill: the view from Viscount Lisle's position before his descent to the green. Swynbourne Stream, and, probably, the edge of Michaelwood in the fifteenth century, runs across the middle of the picture, above the second field.

11. William the Conqueror, from *The Mayor of Bristol's Kalendar*, 1479/80, showing William and his followers in fifteenth-century armour.

12. The road to North Nibley from Berkeley.

Opposite 13. The south aisle of St Martin's, North Nibley, reputedly built by William, Lord Berkeley to give thanks for his victory at Nibley Green.

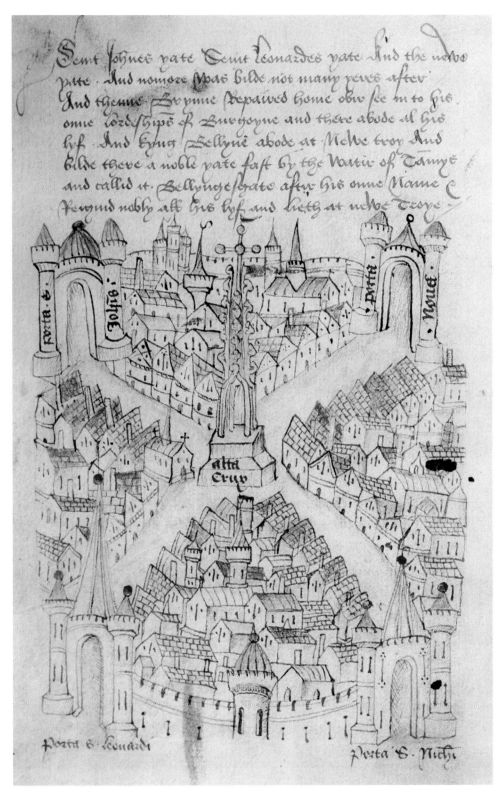

15. Plan of Bristol, from *The Mayor of Bristol's Kalendar*.

Opposite 14. The mayor of Bristol takes office, 1479/80: Mayor William Spencer commissioned *The Mayor of Bristol's Kalendar*, in which this illustration appears.

16–18. Heraldic glass in the Great Hall of Berkeley Castle, recording 'William the Waste All', the capture of the castle in 1452 [*sic*] and the Beauchamp marriage alliance.

JOHN (TALBOT)
1st vicount LISLE of KINGSTON LISLE
son of 1st EARL of SHREWSBURY
took CASTLE by treachery 1452. James
the 1st recovered it in 1455.

Opposite top 19. The inner gatehouse of Berkeley Castle. According to Grantley Berkeley, Lord Berkeley's men assembled in the courtyard before marching to Nibley Green.

Opposite bottom 20. 'The Battle of Nibley Green', a colourful interpretation by local artist Robert Hollingworth, which is very much in the spirit of Grantley Berkeley's novel.

21. The sunken lane leading from Nibley Green. According to Grantley Berkeley, this was the site of a massacre of Lisle's fleeing troops.

22. Grantley Berkeley's Druid Oak, the fictional muster point for Berkeley's men.

lors – should have taken the time to compose what is a reasonably polished response, over three times the length of Lisle's letter.

Berkeley's letter contains a detailed and damning indictment of Lisle's behaviour; Lisle's, on the other hand, carries only the imputation that his opponent had no right to his title, and that he had been spreading rumours about Lisle's intended use of Welsh retainers. Lisle's first point was the basis of the dispute, well known as an accusation levelled at Berkeley by his enemies, and so unlikely to have been particularly embarrassing. The second, by forcing Lisle to deny such plans, and bringing to mind his Welsh connections, may have worked against the viscount's reputation. Lisle's opening sneer, 'I marveill ye come not forth with all thy Carts of gunnes, bowes, with oder ordinance, that ye set forward to come to my manor of Wotton to bete it down upon my head', far from being an imputation of cowardice, can be read as evidence of Berkeley's restraint: he has the means with which to reduce Lisle's stronghold, but so far has refused to employ them. Lisle then provokes Berkeley to combat, presenting him with a challenge that he was honour-bound to accept. In short, Lisle's letter does not cast its composer in a very positive light. Therefore, it is not impossible that this was a subtle piece of propaganda emanating from the Berkeley camp. Likewise, the documents relating to the January plot might strike an enthusiast for conspiracy theories as being just a little too convenient, implicating not only disgraced members of the Berkeley household but also Lisle himself in a distinctly sordid affair which could almost have been designed to rekindle memories of the Talbots' equally underhand capture of Berkeley Castle in 1451. As we have seen, the probability that Maurice King, one of the alleged January plotters, remained in Berkeley service until at least 1472 also raises suspicions that, even if the text is not itself a forgery, it does not tell the whole story. Leaving aside the unlikely possibility of the original documents coming to light, there seems no way in which these theories could be proved or disproved.

Reconstructing the battle itself is difficult. Apart from their detailed and gory descriptions of the murders, the two King's Bench suits supply only places and times: Viscount Lisle was killed at ten o'clock on the morning of 20 March at Nibley Green; John Lewis met his fate on the same day, in the same place, but an hour later. Neither mention that the killings took place during the course of a battle. Given that the affair was illegal, it is perhaps not surprising that neither plaintiff wished to dwell on the circumstances that brought their husbands to Nibley Green on that day. In addition, presenting their murders as unprovoked attacks in cold blood made the crimes seem all the more heinous. Our major sources for the events of the battle itself are local and family traditions, recorded by Smyth, but also by the early Tudor antiquary John Leland, and his Elizabethan counterpart William Camden, together with the testimony from the two cases heard before the court of King's Bench. Writing in the early 1540s, John Leland, antiquarian and traveller, made two references to Nibley Green. In a section of his *Itinerary* dealing with Gloucestershire, Leland notes how,

> Ther was great harte burning betwixt the Lorde Berkeley and the Lorde Lisle for the maner of Wotton under Egge, in so much that they pointed to fight, and meting yn a medow at a place caullid Nebley, Berkeley's archers sodainly shotte sore, and the Lord Lisle lifteting up the visar of his helme was by an archer of the forest of Dene shotte in at the mouth and oute of the nek: and a few beside beyng slayn Lisle menne fled.

Leland returned to the subject a little later in the same section:

> There hath been a very greate campe of menne of warre on an hille now caullyd Nebley over growen with wodde... The Lord Lisle was slayn with an arow by one James Hiatte of the forest of Deene yn Nebley paroch.[22]

Leland's account, written over seventy-five years before Smyth's, and apparently unknown to him, appears to offer impressive confirmation of the latter's version of events in all but the identity of Lisle's killer (we shall return to this topic later). A note of caution is necessary, however. For local traditions to have survived for Smyth to record them, they must, of course, have been available to Leland as well. He would still have heard these stories at least thirty-five years after the event: plenty of time for the tale to grow in the telling. The detail that the two lords 'pointed to fight' could have been derived from the roll in the Berkeley Castle muniment room.

Camden's account, contained in his *Britannia*, is terse, and tells us little about the battle:

> ...Wotton under Edge, which yet remembreth the slaughter of Sir Thomas Talbot Viscount Lisle, here slain in the time of King Edward 4. in an encounter with the Lord Barkley, about possessions, since which time hath continued suits between their Posterity until now lately they were finally compounded.[23]

Smyth knew of Camden's work, and quotes this section in his own.

Smyth's approach to oral tradition combines fascination, caution, but perhaps also credulity.[24] He writes,

> And if traditions might bee here allowed, I would assure this noble family, That within thirty two years last, by reason of my dwelling at Nibley, and of my oft resort to Wotton and to the villages adjoyning, I have often heard many old men and weomen in those places [and here he gives the names of eleven of them]... many of whose parents lived in the time of king Edward the fourth, and most of themselves were born in the time of king Henry the seaventh, as their leases and copies declared, some of them one hundred and ten yeares old, divers an hundred, and none under fourscore, relate the reports of their parents kinsfolks and neighbours present at this skirmish, some with the one lord, and others with the other; and of such as carryed victuals and weapons to some of those companies,... and after climbed up trees, (being then boys of twelve and sixteen yeares,) to see the battle...

The accounts given by his venerable neighbours Smyth judged,

> not possible almost by such plaine Country people to be fained... insomuch as I cannot otherwise but deliver them as truths; and much the rather for the full discourse thereof which old Mr Charles Hiet, (whose great grandfather James is one of the Def[endan]ts in the said appeale,) had with the lord Henry Berkeley at Berkeley Castle the 25th of September. 1603, which my self then heard soe perticularly delivered from the relation of his father and grandfather as if the same had been but yesterday: the said lord Henry himself seconding most of what Mr Hiet related, from the records of divers others made to himselfe in his youth, some of whom were then born and of the age of discretion, as his L[or]d[shi]pp then affirmed...

At this point, however, Smyth the lawyer's scepticism reasserts itself:

> But enough of these traditions and reports, wherein I have exceeded mine own Inclination because this passage is of most remarkableness in this family.

Smyth's claims for the longevity of some of his neighbours defy belief, unless the sixteenth-century Vale of Berkeley was some kind of Shangri-La. Writing in 1618, Smyth tells us that his meetings with these ancients had taken place less than thirty-two years earlier. Had they been born during the reign of Henry VII (1485–1509), as he claimed, then they would have been over seventy-seven years of age at the time of the interviews. This would indeed have been a remarkable age for the time, but not impossible. Their parents may well have been born before Edward IV's reign ended in 1483, and it is possible that a five-year-old boy, scrambling in the branches to watch the fighting, could have fathered one of Smyth's informants at the age of forty-four in 1509, but that there were as many as eleven children of the Nibley Green generation alive in 1586 for Smyth to interview is unlikely, to say the least. Smyth was not by nature gullible, and his confusion is probably explained by the uncertainty in ascertaining the ages of those born before records of baptism were regularly kept.

Four hundred years on, we are in a far worse position than Smyth to decide upon the veracity of these tales, and they should be given their due consideration alongside what scraps of evidence we have from the documentary record. Smyth claims that his informants told him of how their ancestors supplied Berkeley's army as it,

> lay close in the utter skirts of Michaellwood chace, out of which this lord Berkeley brake, when hee first beheld the lord Lisle with his fellow-ship discending down that hill from Nibley Church... And how the lord Berkeleys number was about one thousand, and exceeded the other in greatness: that the place of stand was at fowleshard, whence this lord Will[ia]m sent upon the lord Lisle the first shower of his arrowes; That one Black Will, (soe called) should shoot the lord Lisle, as his beaver was up; And that Thomas Longe father of the said Will[ia]m [one of Smyth's informants] was servant to one of them who helped to carry the lord Lisle when hee was slayne... And that a spetial man of the lord Lisles company was then also slaine, and buryed under the great stone tomb which yet remaines in the south side of Nibley Church yard.

Literary and record sources for the deployment of forces and the course of the battle are sparse and problematic. Luckily, the general topography of Nibley Green appears to have changed little since 1470 – at least, the battlefield has not disappeared under a housing estate or car park – and the landscape itself can provide valuable evidence.[25]

Nibley Green extends around Shankley Hill, on which stands the village and church of North Nibley. The green was created around 1300 as one of the

22. Shankley Hill from Nibley Green: the view from Lord Berkeley's position at the edge of Michaelwood Chase.

assarts carved out of Michaelwood (the 'mickle', or 'great' wood) by the second Lord Thomas Berkeley. Michaelwood Chase lay to the south-west of Shankley Hill: its borders have gradually receded over the centuries, but in 1470 it probably extended as far as the Swynebourne Stream. Had Berkeley's men issued from Michaelwood, as Smyth records, then the battle would have taken place in the south-western part of the green. Lisle was marching towards Nibley Green from Wotton-under-Edge, and the road ran along the top of Shankley Hill, through the village. Lisle's force would have been positioned first at the top of Shankley Hill before descending to the green. Smyth names 'Fowleshard' as the scene of the fighting. The place-name element 'hard' usually refers to a firm piece of land in the midst of marsh or bog. The Swynebourne Stream often makes the southern part of the green very boggy. Fowles Grove – presumably the same place – is recorded in medieval deeds as covering about seven acres. Fowles Hard, or Grove, does not appear on maps, but Foley's Grove, which does, may be a corruption of this place name: in 1300 Lord Thomas Berkeley granted land in this area which had once belonged to William Fowell, who may have been the original of 'Foley'. Foley's Grove, now known as Nibley Grove, is a small copse next to the road leading to Bush Farm.

This was the battleground selected by William Lord Berkeley. At first sight, it does not appear well-chosen. Lisle, on Shankley Hill, had the advantage of

23. The modern road from Wotton-under-Edge to North Nibley: the route taken by Lisle's army.

height. No deployment on the green could escape his gaze. His forces were well beyond bowshot of any archers deployed at the edge of Michaelwood, and to move within effective range would have exposed them to Lisle's archers, who had the benefit of shooting down the slope. The site appeared to offer Lisle all the advantages; in fact, Lisle may have walked into a trap.

Berkeley had appointed eight in the morning as the time of their meeting. In mid-March in this part of England the sun rises at around six, giving Berkeley two hours of daylight to reach Nibley Green from Berkeley Castle, five miles (8km) away. The King's Bench pleas give ten and eleven as the hours at which fighting took place: clocks were scarce (was there a clock on Nibley Church tower?) and telling the time accurately by other means was difficult, so we should probably not make too much of the difference of one hour. However, this testimony does suggest that there may have been a delay of up to three hours between the arrival of the two forces and the outbreak of hostilities. Was this time spent goading, or persuading, Lisle down from Shankley Hill?

Shankley Hill rises eighty metres above Nibley Green and its south-western slope has a one-in-five gradient. Standing at its summit, Lisle was in an almost

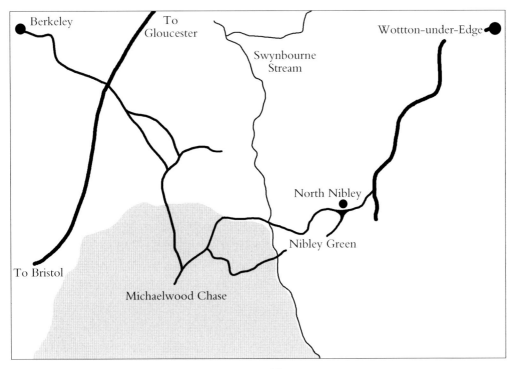

24. Routes to Nibley Green.

impregnable position. Why did he surrender it? There are two possible answers. The first is that Berkeley asked him to come down, and he agreed. This might sound incredible, but it would have been entirely in keeping with chivalric concepts of honour. Lisle, if we are to believe that the text of his challenge is genuine, had called for this battle, and the onus was on him to conduct himself in a manner that ensured a fair and honourable fight. Expecting his opponent to labour up Shankley Hill under showers of arrows would not have been regarded as fair and honourable. Berkeley could have refused to give battle in these circumstances, and he would have received a favourable hearing had he then blamed the non-event on Lisle's cowardice, not his own.

The second explanation is that Lisle moved onto Nibley Green because he thought it would bring him a tactical advantage. This is conceivable if what he saw below him was a smaller force than his own, and he believed that he could sweep it off the field with the impetus of a downhill charge. Smyth believed that Berkeley's force was the larger, and this would seem to be borne out by what we know of those individuals who were present. Smyth records the tradition that Berkeley's men broke from the cover of Michaelwood when

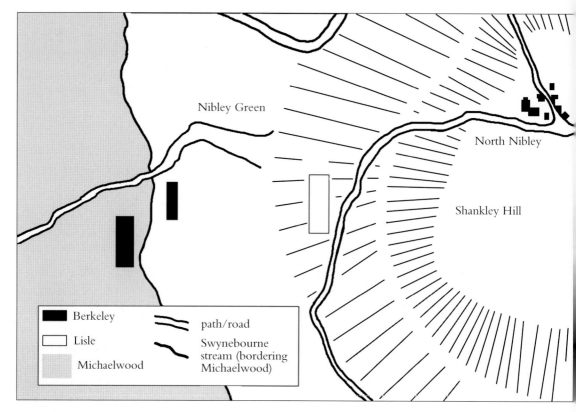

25. Possible deployment of forces at Nibley Green.

they saw Lisle's force coming down the hill: if true, this might seem to invalidate the first explanation, since it implies that Lisle was unaware of their presence when he began his descent. However, he must have known that at least some of Berkeley's men were present, if we are to believe Smyth's story of local people supplying Berkeley's force as it lay in the woods, since these victuallers would have been visible from Lisle's position, and anyway, he was of course expecting Berkeley's men to be there. What drew him down may have been a smaller body of men, deployed by Berkeley for this very purpose in front of Michaelwood, and perhaps behind the Swynebourne Stream. This would have been a detachment, big enough to convince Lisle that it constituted Berkeley's entire army, and perhaps bearing aloft his banner. Berkeley may have had this tactic already in mind the day before, when composing his response to Lisle's challenge (again, assuming it to be genuine). Noting Lisle's demand 'that I should bee there with all the power that I could make', he went on to assure his opponent that, 'I will not bring the tenth part that I can make...'. Was this 'tenth part' destined to be the bait in Berkeley's trap?

Howe the Dolphyn of ffraunce leude in the Ner 6ᵗⁱ men of Armes w̃ the
Erles of Sando̅ s hensh̃n and bothe the frenysh̃ y̅ rles were slayn and y̅ᵗ
of his men beked is slayn all th̃e put to flight And Erle Richard stode
on the sand Erlis his none hande

26. English archers in action.

73

Believing this detachment to be the entire enemy force, perhaps assuming that Berkeley's reinforcements had not yet reached him, Lisle may have seized what he took to be his golden opportunity, and charged down the hill. The steep descent may have caused some disorder among his troops. They would have been further impeded by the soft ground as they neared Swynebourne Stream, and by this time they would have been under arrow shot. The maximum effective range of a bow was about 180 metres. A competent archer could discharge ten arrows a minute.[26] Assuming that Lisle's men, advancing on foot across difficult terrain, and moving only as fast as their heavily armoured leaders, were walking at between two and three miles per hour, they would have been under arrow shot for three to four minutes: time enough to receive as many as forty volleys. They would have taken significant casualties as they advanced across Nibley Green. Once engaged with the forward detachment, Lisle's men could not have broken off in good order if they discovered that they had walked into an ambush as the rest of Berkeley's army appeared out of the trees.

Alternatively, Lisle's force may not even have got as far as engaging with the enemy. The testimonies of Leland, Smyth and Margaret Viscountess Lisle agree that Lisle was shot early in the encounter, and Leland believed that soon after this his army fled. This is entirely likely, since even in the most professional and well-disciplined of medieval armies the death of the commander could have fatal consequences for morale, resulting in a panic-stricken rout. Lisle's force would have been composed largely of tenants, whose main aim on the day was not to get killed. Seeing their master go down, and faced with superior numbers, their most likely reaction would have been flight. Lisle's death was the decisive event of the battle, as well as being a turning point in the wider saga of the Berkeley dispute. How exactly did it happen?

Both Leland and Smyth recount the story that Lisle was hit by an arrow in the face, and the latter adds the detail that this occurred 'as his beaver was up'. The bevor, or *mentonnière,* was a protection for the neck and lower part of the face made from two or three riveted plates, and was worn to supplement the sallet, a rounded helmet that covered the head but left the lower part of the face exposed.[27] Leland's claim that Lisle was 'shotte in at the mouth and oute of the nek' would seem to support the notion that he had his bevor undone, even though Leland uses the word 'visor'. Fifteenth-century men-at-arms often removed their bevors, which chafed the neck and restricted breathing, but Smyth's claim that Lisle's bevor 'was up' suggests that he is employing the word 'beaver' to mean visor: a bevor cannot be raised, a visor can. This would match Leland's use of the word, although he may have actually had a bevor in

27. Italian composite armour, 1440–80, with a sallet and bevor, of the type possibly worn by Viscount Lisle at Nibley Green (Royal Armouries, Leeds, II.168; copyright The Board of Trustees of the Armouries).

mind! This would mean that Lisle was wearing either a very up-to-date sallet with a moveable visor, or else an armet, a helmet that enclosed the entire head with large cheek pieces hinged to a skull cap, and with a visor covering the face. Both types of helmet, with their visors lowered, gave excellent protection, but this came at the cost of restricting vision and hearing and producing an effect not unlike having one's head in a pressure cooker! Lisle would not have wanted to lower his visor until the last possible moment, and may well have left it up as he negotiated the muddy terrain of Nibley Green. Leland notes how 'Berkeley's archers sodainly shotte sore', suggesting that Lisle was surprised, perhaps by archers hidden in the woods, before he had time to lower his visor.

Smyth records the tradition 'That one Black Will, (soe called) should shoot the lord Lisle'; while Leland's version has it that 'The Lord Lisle was slayn with an arow by one James Hiatte of the forest of Deene'. Black Will has exerted a good deal of fascination down the centuries, and his existence, and role in Lisle's death, has sometimes been taken as fact, even by professional historians, but such claims rest entirely with the local tradition that Smyth recounted, without committing himself to its veracity. James Hiatte, or Hyett, on the

28. Italian armet, Milan, about 1450, of a type possibly worn by Viscount Lisle at Nibley Green (Royal Armouries, Leeds, IV.498; copyright The Board of Trustees of the Armouries).

other hand, we know to have been a real person, and what is more, to have been present at Nibley Green.

In her King's Bench suit, Margaret Talbot claimed that Lisle had been shot in the left side of the face by an arrow from one archer, while a second shot him in the right side of the face, both arrows penetrating as far as the brain; after he had fallen, he was stabbed in the right side of the body, the blade reaching his heart. As accessories to this murder she named William Lord Berkeley, his brothers Maurice and Thomas Berkeley esquires, James Hyett, Richard Hylpe and John Sawnders. The men Margaret named as the archers were John Beley, a husbandman (tenant farmer) of Paganhill, and John Body, who is described as a painter from Bristol. While it is quite possible that a brawny husbandman might also be an expert shot, a town-dwelling painter, whether of the artistic or decorating variety, does not immediately strike one as such promising material. The man she accused of striking the *coup de grâce*, John Bendall, was from Berkeley, and a yeoman, and therefore of slightly more elevated social status than Beley. Leland's candidate as Lisle's killer, James Hyett, constable of St Briavel's Castle and an esquire, is highly unlikely to have been wielding a bow: he would have been among the armoured men-at-arms. However, the killer could well have been part of his Forest of Dean contingent, particularly since that region was famous for producing excellent archers. Neither Beley nor Body seem to have had links with the Forest of Dean, and look unlikely candidates. Margaret's claim that Lisle was killed by three men might seem like a typical plaintiff's attempt to implicate as many people as possible, and her choice of individuals to accuse of his murder may have had more to do with pre-existing grudges, or simply the calculation of who was least able to defend himself, than any sure knowledge of the real assailant. Had Lisle fallen during an arrow shower there would have been any number of archers with an equal claim to the dubious honour of his killing. Her version contradicts Leland's account of the nature of Lisle's injuries (and supports the notion that Lisle had his visor raised, with the arrows perhaps entering through his eyes), but much more importantly, she claims that her husband was hit by two archers, presumably simultaneously. What are we to make of this? Possibly, the sound of the first volley of an intensive arrow shower caused the inexperienced Lisle to look up instinctively, with his helmet unfastened, and thereby received two arrows in the face before he fell to the ground. But Margaret's version of the story, if we are to believe it, sounds more like her husband was targeted at close range: to receive one arrow in the face is a misfortune; two sounds like assassination. With the memory still raw of his mother's supposed murder, and, possibly, of the attempt on his own life by

Lisle's grandmother, Lord Berkeley may have been perfectly capable of arranging his opponent's murder. Multiple arrow wounds to the face were far from unknown in later medieval warfare. At the first battle of St Albans the duke of Buckingham was hit by three arrows in the face, but he may also have been deliberately targeted.[28] Smyth's story 'that a spetial man of the lord Lisles company' was slain with his master probably refers to Lisle's personal bodyguard: he might have proved invaluable in a mêlée with Berkeley's men-at-arms, but he could have done nothing to protect his charge against Berkeley's archers.

John Lewis was the other victim of Nibley Green to whom we can put a name. His widow's plea before King's Bench names his murderers as: John Daunt, whose bill cleaved his forehead to the brain; John Draycot, who struck him in the back; and Robert Tanner, who also gave him a mortal wound. Accessories to this murder were named as Thomas Tanner, David Jones, Nicholas Jones and Thomas Halyday. John Lewis had been fighting for Berkeley.[29] Both of these King's Bench suits therefore indicate that there was hand-to-hand fighting at Nibley Green, and while Lisle could have been finished off after his men had deserted him, the manner in which Lewis was despatched (and here we are assuming – possibly rashly – that his widow's testimony is accurate) raises further questions about the course of the battle. He may have been pursuing Lisle's men during their rout, and was unlucky enough to become isolated and picked off, but it is more likely that his death occurred during a mêlée that preceded the rout. If we are correct in assuming that knowledge of Lisle's fall would have been sufficient to cause his men to break off, then Lewis's death suggests that Lisle was brought down just before the two sides came together, so that news of this event did not have time to travel through the ranks. Given the small size of Lisle's force, it could not have taken long for his men to realise that he was on the ground. This possibility may support the theory that Lisle was the victim of an assassin's arrow, with crack shots deployed to target Lisle at close range during, or immediately prior, to the mêlée, but it may also have been the case that Lisle was brought down in the final volley of arrows, discharged as the two sides came within a few yards of each other, and that Berkeley's men were upon their enemies before they had time to flee.

Smyth also recounts how, immediately after the battle, Lord Berkeley and his men pillaged the house at Wotton which the Talbot party had established as their headquarters, and took away those deeds they found there that had a bearing on the property dispute, among them, probably, the papers that the earl and countess of Warwick had removed from Berkeley Castle in 1417.[30]

29. Wotton-under-Edge parish church. Wotton House stood next to the churchyard.

Many of these documents remain, to this day, among the Berkeley muniments. Viscount Lisle's wife – now his widow – Margaret, daughter of William Herbert, earl of Pembroke, was inside Wotton House, awaiting her husband's return. She was also awaiting the birth of their only child, and Smyth relates how, sixteen days after the sacking of Wotton, Margaret suffered a miscarriage: brought on, he is in no doubt, by the events of 20 March. This account is supported by Margaret's own testimony in the case she brought before King's Bench. Here she describes how she was chased from village to village after the battle. With Viscount Lisle dead, and his only child stillborn, the Berkeleys were in the ascendant, having, in the words of Smyth, revenged 'the innocent blood of that virtuous and princely lady Isable... spilt at Gloucester seventeen years before'.[31] They were also able to occupy all the disputed properties. This brought a temporary halt to hostilities.

3

AFTERMATH

For all that Lord Berkeley and Viscount Lisle were engrossed in their own private squabble in the early months of 1470, they could not have been unaware of events beyond the borders of Gloucestershire, for this was a time of particular tumult. The year would end with the deposed Edward IV exiled to Burgundy, and Henry VI back on the throne.[1] The people who put him there were most unlikely allies. In July 1469 Richard Neville, earl of Warwick, 'The Kingmaker', to whom, at least in his own opinion, Edward IV owed his crown, and the king's brother, George, duke of Clarence, stood revealed as the promoters of rebellion in the north. The rebels, led by 'Robin of Redesdale', a member of the Conyers family, loyal Neville retainers, marched south to join forces with the earl and the duke, and at Edgecote, near Banbury in Oxfordshire, the combined host met and defeated a royal army led by William Herbert, earl of Pembroke, and the earl of Devon. Pembroke and his brother Sir Richard Herbert were executed after the battle. Edward IV was captured soon afterwards. Meanwhile, Richard Woodville, Earl Rivers, and his son Sir John Woodville, the father and brother of Queen Elizabeth, were captured at Chepstow and taken to Coventry where, on 12 August, they were executed. On the same day the youngest of Pembroke's brothers, Sir Thomas Herbert, was executed at Bristol, while the earl of Devon was killed at Bridgwater.

Despite what may have appeared a decisive victory, Warwick was unable to rule through Edward as his puppet, and in September he was forced to release him. Six months later, Warwick and Clarence once more raised rebellion, and on 12 March Edward IV defeated the rebel army at Empingham, or Losecote Field. On the day of Nibley Green, Edward was pursuing Warwick and Clarence through the north of England. Eventually, the pair found their way to the West Country. At Bristol Warwick left his artillery, his wife and his daughters in safe keeping, before he and Clarence took ship at Dartmouth and headed for temporary exile in France. Here, Warwick and Clarence sealed an extraordinary pact with their erstwhile enemy, Margaret of Anjou, by which they promised to put her husband back on the throne. With French help this unholy alliance forced Edward to flee once more, and on 3 October 1470 Henry VI was restored, beginning the short-lived Lancastrian Readeption. Warwick had a new puppet, one infinitely more manipulable than Edward IV.

The battle of Nibley Green has traditionally been seen as having little to do with the Wars of the Roses. Usually, it is portrayed as a purely private squabble, its one link with these national events being that they so distracted the king that the feuding lords Berkeley and Lisle were able to take to the battlefield without fear of royal intervention: there was, in Smyth's words, 'noe time to take notice of these Nibley tumults.'[2] There is no doubt that, while the royal cat was away, the baronial mice did play. At around the same time as Nibley Green, outbreaks of serious violence punctuated a number of other magnate or gentry feuds. In August 1469 the duke of Norfolk besieged Caister Castle in Norfolk, held by the Paston family; there were also clashes between the Stanleys and the Harringtons from 1469 to 1471. A similar pattern of private violence erupting during periods of national crisis occurred in the 1450s, and as we have seen, earlier armed clashes between the Berkeleys and their opponents coincided with breakdowns in royal authority.[3]

While Nibley Green cannot be regarded as a 'Wars of the Roses battle', in the sense that it did not involve leading political players and it was not fought to remove or control a king, not all of the participants were disengaged from the factional politics of Lancaster and York. While Smyth believed that his feud with the Talbots prevented Lord Berkeley from 'actuall sidinge with either of the two royall houses of Yorke and Lancaster' which, had he done so, might have had an even more deleterious effect on the family's fortunes than the feud itself, Leland was firmly of the opinion that 'Berkeley favorid Henry the 6. parte. Lisle favorid Edwarde the 4.'[4] The truth probably lies somewhere in-between.

Viscount Lisle did not live long enough to play any significant part in politics, but given that he was married to a daughter of William Herbert, earl of Pembroke, it might be supposed that his sympathies were most definitely Yorkist. Pembroke and Warwick were bitter rivals. However, his most prominent supporter at Nibley Green was a man whose commitment to the cause of Warwick, Clarence and the Readeption of Henry VI is unmistakable. John Daunt was the second son of Nicholas Daunt of Wotton-under-Edge, and appears to have received a legal training. In 1475 the Berkeley brothers alleged that John and his brother Nicholas had been accomplices in their false imprisonment in 1451/2: this may have been the case, since by this time the Daunt brothers were retained by John Talbot, earl of Shrewsbury. Daunt prospered under Henry VI. He was described as a king's serjeant and groom when he was made parker of Mere, in Wiltshire, in 1451. He was a yeoman of the crown from 1452.[5] The Yorkist takeover in 1460/1 shattered this comfortable existence. On 8 January 1461 his arrest was ordered as one of those 'evil-disposed persons, adherents of Henry VI', active in Somerset, Dorset and Wiltshire.[6] His commitment to Lancaster was still strong in 1471: on 14 April, the day that Prince Edward and his mother, Margaret of Anjou, landed at Weymouth, the prince wrote to Daunt, requesting that he join them, 'with all such fellowship as yowe canne make in your moste defensible Aray'. Tradition has it that Queen Margaret slept at his house at Wotton en route for Tewkesbury.[7] He may have fought at the battle. In March 1470 this die-hard Lancastrian seems to have had few qualms about fighting for the son-in-law of one of the most prominent of Yorkist lords. At Nibley Green, it was loyalty to the house of Talbot, rather than to the house of York, that brought John Daunt to battle.

The presence of one Lancastrian among Viscount Lisle's force does not, of itself, tell us anything about Thomas Talbot's political affiliations. His widow's actions in the two years after the battle may provide a clue, however. The extent of Margaret Talbot's loss is reminiscent of that of a heroine or victim of a Greek tragedy: in the space of less than a year she had lost her father, two uncles, her husband and their only child, all, directly or indirectly, as the result of political violence. While it would not be surprising if Margaret herself had been plunged into despair and inactivity by the scale of her personal catastrophe, someone, somewhere, was moving quickly after her husband's death. Writs of *diem clausit extremum*, ordering enquiries into the lands of the late viscount, were issued to the escheators in ten counties on 28 March, a mere eight days after Nibley Green, and on 6 April, before all the inquisitions *post mortem* had been held, his sisters, Elizabeth, aged eighteen, and Margaret, aged sixteen, were named as his heirs in letters patent and allowed to enter his lands. No reference was made at this time to their husbands, but at some point Elizabeth was married to Edward Grey of Astley, and Margaret to Sir George Vere, brother of the earl of Oxford. Both men were Warwick adherents, and after Edward IV's return both suffered attainder, and their property was settled on the Talbot sisters. If, as seems likely, the sisters were married during the Readeption, then we are perhaps justified in seeing this as something akin to a hostile takeover of the Lisle inheritance by the Neville faction. Margaret did not receive her dower (of the manors of Painswick, Gloucestershire, Norton Beauchamp, Somerset and Limpsham, Dorset) until November 1471, six months after the fall of the Readeption regime. Without her dower, or at least the immediate prospect of its acquisition, Margaret would probably have found it difficult to mount legal action against Lord Berkeley, which raises the possibility that he had some hand in delaying its assignment to her.[8]

In medieval England it was usually up to the victim to initiate the legal processes that might – the chances were not great – result in successful prosecution and punishment of the guilty. The paralysing effects of personal tragedy and her lack of dower may explain why Margaret does not appear to have sought redress from the courts soon after her husband's murder. However, Margaret waited until June/July 1471 before bringing her suit to the court of King's Bench. She would not receive her dower for at least another four months, so the delay of over a year was not simply the result of lack of resources. Instead, it is likely to have been related to wider political events. Margaret's inaction during the six months immediately following her husband's death could well be explained, in whole or in part, by her personal circumstances. But this was also a time of great political uncertainty which continued into the following period of the Readeption. That Margaret waited until summer 1471, until, in other words, Edward IV was firmly back on the throne, suggests that she thought the chances of justice from an administration dominated by the Warwick-Clarence-Lancastrian axis were so slim as to render pointless any attempts at securing legal redress. To understand why she might have come to this conclusion, we need to consider Lord Berkeley's political affiliations.

Berkeley's treatment by Edward IV after his triumph in 1471 was exceptional. He was removed from the county bench, and would not sit again as a justice of the peace until May 1475.[9] Of the local lay JPs who had served on the Gloucestershire bench during Edward's first reign, Lord Berkeley was among only three who were not appointed in the first commission of his second reign, in June 1471.[10] For a man of Berkeley's local standing to be left off his county bench for four years could only have been seen as a very public, and very humiliating, rebuke. After his return Edward's policy had to be one of reconciliation: only the most die-hard Lancastrians were targeted. Only towards the end of 1472 did he embark upon a general realignment of the Gloucestershire bench.[11] Berkeley's rehabilitation was slow. On 20 January 1472 he was granted a general pardon for all offences committed before 14 January; he took out another pardon on 20 May.[12] Despite this, he would not be allowed to participate in royal commissions until February 1474, when he was appointed to a commission of array in Gloucestershire.[13] For nearly three years the leading resident magnate in Gloucestershire was excluded from that county's local governance.

Lord Berkeley's brothers, Maurice and Thomas, appear to have shared in his disgrace. Smyth recounts how 'That for his sake and in his quarrell, both their lives were soe farr indangered That they stood outlawed for felony, and ranne the hazard of an appeale of murder, strongly prosecuted'; Maurice had lived at Thornbury until the battle of Nibley Green, 'for which fellonious fact [his participation in the battle], hee was outlawed, and inforced for some time after, (till peace was made and pardon procured,) to withdraw himself and leave Thornbury... whither after hee returned and for many yeares remained.'[14] Maurice's rehabilitation, like his eldest brother's, seems to have waited until 1474, in which year he was retained by William, Lord Hastings. Hastings was Edward IV's trusted deputy in the Midlands, and his large retinue can be seen, in the 1470s, as an extension of royal power and patronage. At about the same time, Lord Berkeley granted an annuity of £5 to Hastings, perhaps as *quid pro quo* for his patronage of Maurice.[15]

If Berkeley's harsh treatment after Edward's return in 1471 was simply a reaction to his involvement in Lisle's murder, then this would strongly suggest that Berkeley's version of events leading up to the battle, as recorded in the letters of the January conspirators and the challenge and response, all copied onto the roll now preserved in the Berkeley muniments, failed in its intended purpose of convincing the authorities that he was forced into giving battle by Lisle's challenge to his honour. An enthusiast for chivalry like Edward IV would surely have had some sympathy with Berkeley's predica- ment, if he believed it to have been genuine. Leland's claim that 'Berkeley to wyn after [the battle of Nibley Green] Kinge Eduarde's good Wylle promised to make the Marquise of Dorset his Heire but that succeded not' is intriguing.[16] Thomas Grey, Marquis of Dorset, was the son of Elizabeth Woodville's first husband, Sir John Grey, and therefore Edward IV's step-son. If Berkeley did make the offer he must have been desperate to placate the king, since while he did not yet have any children of his own, the move would have disinherited his eldest brother Maurice, who had risked life and livelihood in his cause. If true, Leland's story is also interesting in the light of what was to come. Dorset's brother, Sir Edward Grey, would soon emerge as a troublesome claimant to the disputed Lisle properties, and Berkeley would indeed disinherit his brother Maurice. Perhaps then, Leland's account is no more than a garbled version of these events. In any case, even if Berkeley had done nothing else to incite Edward's wrath, his subsequent disgrace would seem to imply that the king held him in some way responsible for initiating the chain of events that would lead to the young viscount's miserable death at Nibley Green.

Lisle's death was not, however, Berkeley's only offence. In the six months of national crisis between Nibley Green and Edward's flight on 29 September 1470 there was probably little opportunity for the king to attend to events in Gloucestershire. Six days after Nibley Lord Berkeley was among those commissioned to array men to defend the county against Warwick and Clarence, but since Viscount Lisle was also included on this commission news of the battle had clearly not reached the ears of the king. The royal bureaucracy may only have known of Lisle's death, though not necessarily the manner of it, by 28 March, when the writs of *diem clausit extremum* were issued.[17] Whatever disquiet may have been felt at Berkeley's actions at Nibley was not sufficient to bring about his removal from the county bench in the final six months before Edward's deposition.

From December 1470 until its end, Lord Berkeley was a supporter of the Readeption regime. While he was missing from the first Readeption justice commission, on 11 December 1470, this omission was rectified nine days later, and he continued to sit on the Gloucestershire bench until Edward's return. On 16 January 1471 Lord Berkeley was part of a commission of *oyer et terminer* in Gloucestershire, headed by Jasper Tudor, the Lancastrian earl of Pembroke.[18] Berkeley's appointments as JP and commissioner of *oyer et terminer* are significant, because the Readeption government relied on a small group of trusted individuals: those given such responsibilities in the shires are likely to have been either adherents of Warwick or Clarence, or to have harboured Lancastrian loyalties.[19] The short-lived Readeption came to an end at Tewkesbury on 4 May 1471. Two days earlier, Margaret of Anjou and her army had arrived at Berkeley. They probably got there at about 5.00 p.m. Very likely they spent the night there, and if so, then it is equally likely that the castle played host to Margaret and her close companions, including her son, Prince Edward, his wife, Anne Neville, Edmund Beaufort, duke of Somerset, John Courtenay, earl of Devon, and John, Lord Wenlock. Was Lord Berkeley present? Had he been, and faced with an army of about 6,000, he would have had little choice but to extend his hospitality to these Lancastrian notables. How sincere his welcome would have been we shall never know. By then he would probably have learnt of Warwick's defeat and death at Barnet on 14 April, eighteen days earlier. Margaret and her commanders had known since the day after the battle, but had decided to carry on regardless.[20] Whatever his political sympathies, Berkeley would have played host with a heavy heart: Margaret's chances did not look good. If the Yorkists won, even if his actions at Nibley Green and his record under the Readeption had not already compromised him in their eyes, accommodating the remaining Lancastrian

30. St Briavel's Castle, Forest of Dean. The castle is now a youth hostel, owned by English Heritage.

leadership in his own castle surely would. One wonders if any of Berkeley's men were persuaded to join the Lancastrians on their march to Tewkesbury, and even if Lord Berkeley himself, or his brothers, might have been among them. If so, one further speculation is irresistible: did John Daunt and the Berkeleys find themselves fighting shoulder to shoulder against the Yorkists, just over a year since they had been trying to kill each other at Nibley Green?

The political careers of some of Lord Berkeley's associates support the impression of a man whose loyalty to the Yorkists was at best dubious – although, of course, John Daunt's example warns us against too easy an association between the political loyalties of lord and retainer. Apart from his brothers, foremost among Lord Berkeley's contingent at Nibley Green was James Hyett esquire. Hyett was high in royal favour at the start of Edward IV's reign. In February 1462, described as one of the king's servitors, he was granted manors forfeited from Lancastrians in Oxfordshire, Wiltshire and Somerset, and the following month he was appointed constable of St Briavel's Castle, in the Forest of Dean, for life. He was a subsidy collector in Gloucestershire in June 1468.[21] One year later, however, he had thrown in his lot with the emergent opposition led by Warwick and Clarence. Both had an interest in the manor and castle of St Briavel's, and Clarence held the farm of the royal revenues from the Forest of Dean until his execution in 1478. St Briavel's Castle was the administrative centre of the Forest.[22] Hyett's appointment as constable would have brought him into the duke's orbit, if he was not already part of Clarence's affinity, but his links with Warwick may have been even closer. In July 1469, having married his daughter Isabel to Clarence in his Calais stronghold, Warwick landed in Kent with the intention of challenging Edward, who at that point was in the North attempting to deal with Robin of Redesdale's rebellion – a rebellion, of course, that had been encouraged by Warwick. Soon after his landfall in England, Warwick sent a letter to Hyett, commanding him to come to his assistance.[23] He was not to be disappointed. Margaret Talbot was not the only widow to accuse Hyett of complicity in her husband's death. In the summer of 1470 Jacquetta, duchess of Bedford, brought a suit before King's Bench accusing Warwick and his adherents of the murder of her husband, Richard Woodville, Earl Rivers, in August 1469. Among the accomplices were James Hyett, esquire, of Lydney and Micheldean, a yeoman and four husbandmen of Chepstow, and William Berkeley esquire, of Weoley in Worcestershire.[24] Hyett and the Chepstow men were presumably responsible for Rivers' capture in the vicinity of the town; William Berkeley esquire may also have been involved in this incident. The Berkeleys of Weoley were distant cousins of the lords of Berkeley Castle. By 1469 the Weoley Berkeleys had attached themselves to the Warwick affinity, and would remain loyal to the earl during the Readeption.[25] James Hyett's rehabilitation seems to have taken place at about the same time as the Berkeley brothers. While he purchased a pardon on 30 November 1471, it is not until 1474 that he begins to appear once more on commissions. In February 1475 the constableship of St Briavel's was re-granted to him for life, with the addition that his son Roger would inherit the office on his father's death.[26]

However, the career of John Cassey demonstrates that not everyone who fought for Berkeley at Nibley Green was declared *persona non grata* by the Yorkists. As we saw in the last chapter, Cassey received an annuity from Lord Berkeley for his services at the battle. His father may have been a Talbot councillor, since John Cassey, esquire of Wightfield, Gloucestershire, had been retained in this capacity by Shrewsbury in 1443. If so, the son obviously switched sides.[27] John Cassey was a Gloucestershire JP from 1468; while he was omitted from the Readeption bench commissioned in December 1470, this is because he had been sheriff of the county since November 1469, having been reappointed on 9 October 1470, a week after Edward IV fled from England. He was still sheriff in June 1471. At the same time his brother, William Cassey, was escheator for Gloucestershire.[28] Neither his involvement at Nibley Green nor his collaboration with the Readeption regime seem to have blighted his career after Tewkesbury: he continued as a JP, and was appointed to at least one Gloucestershire commission in each year from 1472 to 1474. In the first of these, a commission of array, he was joined by the duke of Clarence, among others, and in 1471 he witnessed a deed for John Twynyho and his wife Agnes of Cirencester. John Twynyho provides another link between Cassey, Berkeley and Clarence, since he was one of the feoffees to Berkeley Castle and the other disputed properties in 1466 and 1472, to which latter deed Cassey appeared as witness; Twynyho was also a member of Clarence's legal council and a ducal estate official. Cassey may have owed his somewhat charmed existence to the protection of the duke.[29]

Richard Beauchamp of Powick, another of Berkeley's men who was probably present at Nibley, had strong links with Warwick, and also with Clarence, being steward of his Gloucestershire estates. He accompanied Berkeley on the Gloucestershire bench throughout the Readeption, but fought for Edward at Tewkesbury, where he was knighted. Unlike Berkeley, both Beauchamp and Cassey seem to have followed Clarence's lead by changing sides in time, and profitably. Beauchamp, however, did not enjoy untroubled relations with the duke's affinity thereafter.[30]

As we have seen, Philip Mede and John Shipward probably led a contingent of Bristol men to fight for Lord Berkeley at the battle of Nibley Green, and the town's sympathy for Edward IV's enemies was becoming apparent as early as 1469. In this year, after Pembroke's defeat at Edgecote, his brother, Sir Thomas Herbert, was brought to Bristol and executed, probably on the orders of Clarence or Warwick, and they received assistance from Bristol as they fled from Edward's wrath into temporary exile. The town's loyalties were clearly demonstrated in April 1471 when it gave substantial assistance to Margaret of Anjou's army on its way to defeat at Tewkesbury with both money, supplies, artillery and men: the inclusion of Nicholas Hervey, Bristol's Recorder, in the list of those slain at Tewkesbury strongly suggests that an official contingent was despatched.[31] For this miscalculation, Bristol had to buy a pardon, which was granted at Coventry eight days after the battle.[32] The record of the pardon notes that it was granted at the behest of the duke of Clarence. The former rebel, under whose influence, doubtless, Bristol had shown early signs of disloyalty, was now the town's saviour, interceding on its behalf with his brother the king. The irony must have been appreciated, though not with any relish, by the Bristol burgesses as they delved into their purses and swallowed their pride to purchase the pardon. Some leading Bristolians were exempted, presumably because they had been leaders of

Bristol's Lancastrian faction. Among them was the former recorder: while Hervey himself lay dead on the battlefield, his family would still have to suffer retribution for his actions. Another was Philip Mede, Maurice Berkeley's father-in-law and, according to the allegation he had taken such pains to refute, leader, with John Shipward, of the Bristol contingent that had fought at Nibley Green. John Shipward was also exempted. So too was William Spencer, another prominent member of Bristol's governing élite. In or soon after May 1471 Shipward was arrested and his property confiscated. His incarceration lasted until September, when he bought a pardon. But two months later he and Spencer were bound in £100 to appear before the king and council. Their answers were presumably satisfactory, since Spencer received his pardon in December, but he was unable to shake off the slur left by his actions during the Readeption. On 12 March 1479 the king's customs collector in Bristol, Thomas Norton, accused William Spencer, now mayor, of having been a traitor to Edward IV.

The precise nature of Norton's accusation is not recorded, but one of his associates claimed that Spencer had illegally withheld goods worth £700 which had been the property of Warwick and Clarence, and which Norton had been commissioned to confiscate. In turn, Norton was alleged to have used his commission to terrorise John Shipward, his father-in-law. The case was brought before the king, who found in Spencer's favour. The recorder, none other than the former Clarence retainer John Twynyho (Clarence had been executed in 1478), was ordered to punish Norton as he saw fit. Twynyho was probably appointed soon after Recorder Hervey's death at Tewkesbury, and he provides another link between Bristol and the affinity of the duke of Clarence.

Another of those exempted from Bristol's 1471 pardon sits rather oddly alongside these councillors and mayors. He was John Body, painter: the same John Body, surely, whom Margaret Talbot alleged had shot her husband at Nibley Green. In such august company, one can only assume that Body, while socially insignificant, had done something exceptional to bring himself under the king's disapproving gaze. That something might have been the assassination of Viscount Lisle. Body seems to have had a history of resistance to the Yorkist regime. In July 1464 the sheriff of Devon was ordered to arrest one John Body, among others, including the notorious Lancastrian die-hard Sir Thomas Fulford, and bring them before the king in Chancery.[33] Assuming this to be the same man, his arrest order would seem to confirm him as a Lancastrian sympathiser, for whom the Readeption promised a return to the comfortable old order.

31. An eighteenth-century view of Beverstone Castle.

While unlikely to have fought for Lord Berkeley at Nibley, the Berkeley feoffees were probably among his confidants, and so their political affiliations in the period 1469 to 1471 are worth investigating.[34] Sir John Greville, a feoffee in 1466, came from a gentry family with interests in Gloucestershire and Warwickshire which had remained loyal to the Berkeleys in the dark days following Lord Thomas's death in 1417. Their association with the Beauchamp and Neville earls of Warwick was as long lasting: John was a life annuitant of Richard Neville, earl of Warwick, and was also associated with Clarence.[35] Another of the 1466 feoffees, William Langley, had close links not only with the Berkeleys but also with John Twynyho, the Clarence retainer, as revealed by deeds of 1470 and 1471.[36] Twynyho was himself a Berkeley feoffee between 1466 and 1472. Of Lord Berkeley's two distant cousins among his feoffees in 1466, Maurice Berkeley of Beverstone and William Berkeley of Uley, the first remained conspicuously loyal to Edward IV, probably following him into exile in 1470, while the political affiliations of William are unclear. Perhaps significantly, Maurice did not continue as one of Lord Berkeley's feoffees up to 1472.[37] Prominent among the 1466 feoffees were members of the Mowbray connection: Thomas, Lord Stanley, Sir William Stanley, Sir John, later Lord Howard, William Brandon esquire, and

Sir John, Sir Robert and Thomas Wingfield esquire. Of these, Sir William Stanley, Lord Howard and Sir John Wingfield were still in place by 1472. Lord Stanley had been a prominent supporter of Warwick and Clarence at the beginning of the Readeption, but by its end he was no longer completely trusted, and threw in his lot with Edward IV on his return. His younger brother Sir William was not regarded as an ally by the Readeption regime, and gave active support to Edward. Lord Howard, Brandon and the Wingfields also remained loyal to Edward.[38] This is very much a mixed picture, but is it significant that in March 1472, in the depths of Lord Berkeley's disgrace, this rather high-profile group of feoffees transferred their interest in the Berkeley estates to Lord William's brother Thomas and two family retainers, Thomas atte Wood and Maurice King?

Lord Berkeley was probably not a 'Lancastrian' – whatever that may have meant in 1470 – but, if it is possible to know a man by the company he keeps, he was part of the Clarence connection, or at least, on its outer fringes. In fact, this would have been a reasonable assumption, even if we had not been able to associate a number of Berkeley's retainers and associates with the duke's affinity, given Clarence's influence in the area.[39] Before Nibley Green, Berkeley's connections might well have brought him under suspicion from the king. By the time the battle took place, with Edward pursuing Clarence and Warwick across the Midlands, it must have been abundantly clear to Berkeley that a choice would have to be made about which of the two brothers, the king or the duke, to support. Afterwards, with Lisle's blood on his hands, he may have felt that the choice had been made, since now he could look for little favour from Edward.

Lord Berkeley's associations with Clarence would have given protection against any attempt Margaret Talbot may have made to prosecute him, but only until the end of the Readeption. Edward's victory was in large measure made possible by Clarence's shift of allegiance. Political realities made necessary his swift rehabilitation. Berkeley was small fry by comparison, and in any case could hardly be blamed for not keeping up with the duke's mercurial coat-turning. Given the situation in late April and early May 1471, with Margaret of Anjou's army at one point literally camped on his doorstep, a strategic return to the Yorkist fold was in any case probably not an option. Berkeley was left wrong-footed by Edward's rapprochement with his brother and subsequent victory. For Margaret Talbot on the other hand, this was her opportunity, and she was soon pressing her suit in King's Bench.

Margaret began her suit in June/July 1471. The Berkeleys responded with delaying tactics, claiming – correctly – that because the writs issued from the court had been addressed to the sheriff of Gloucestershire they were under no obligation to obey them, since they should have been addressed to the bailiff of the liberty, John Geffreys, and to two of the Berkeley feoffees, Sir Thomas Stanley and Sir Maurice Berkeley; these were therefore summoned to appear, and an enquiry made in the Exchequer as to the justification for this claim. The case was dropped after June 1472.[40]

What Margaret won was compensation, not vengeance. Berkeley and his followers suffered in the purse, not, needless to say, on the executioner's block. If her tactics in the courtroom followed the pattern of many other élite legal actions, then this would have been no more than she expected. The prospect of further expensive and inconvenient legal manoeuvres, and perhaps pressure from the king, persuaded Berkeley to come to terms. In October 1472 Margaret Talbot and William Lord Berkeley and his wife Joan appeared as co-sponsors of a bill presented before parliament, 'for thappesyng of dyvers and many gret varyances, troubles and other exorbytant causes and quarels betwene theym moeved had and of long tyme contynued'. Joan's involvement was made necessary because the lands in question were part of her jointure.[41] Assent was given on 12 October 1472. The Act stated that Lord and Lady Berkeley were to enjoy peaceful possession of Wotton-under-Edge, Simondshall and Erlingham (which had not been one of the properties entailed in 1349), in return for which they were to pay Margaret an annuity of £100 for life. The payments continued until 1482.[42] Another, unstated part of the agreement was doubtless that Margaret would drop her actions against the Berkeleys and their adherents.[43] By August of the following year Margaret was not only in receipt of this annuity, but had also remarried. Her husband was Henry Bodrugan, a Cornish esquire, who would be knighted in 1476. In purely material terms he was a good catch: Bodrugan was on his way to becoming the most powerful man in Cornwall. He was also, without a doubt, the most notorious, with an extraordinarily long and varied list of misdeeds against his name that ranged from rebellion, piracy and murder to probate fraud.[44] Was marriage to this man also part of Margaret's deal with Berkeley, with the latter acting in some way as broker? One hundred pounds a year and a new husband was probably as much as Margaret could have hoped for when she began her campaign for redress. Whether or not we should see this as a happy ending for her it is impossible to say.

Lesser folk might hang for stealing a horse, let alone killing a man; their betters struck deals, paid fines and bought pardons. This was a point brought home in no uncertain terms to Agnes Lewis, the other widow of Nibley Green. Her prosecution of the alleged murderers of her husband John began in February 1471.[45] This of course was during the Readeption, and the timing suggests that, unlike Margaret Talbot, this widow of a Berkeley retainer expected fair treatment under the restored Henry VI. Even after the fall of the Readeption regime, the case seemed at first to be going well. On 12 July 1471 the goods of one of the accused, Nicholas Jones, were granted to John Jones, Nicholas having fled following the murder of John Lewis. Nicholas Jones surrendered and was committed to the Marshalsea, and then bailed by, among others, John Jones, gentleman of Cirencester. In May 1472, Nicholas pleaded not guilty. But this initial progress was not long maintained. The other accused did not respond to repeated summonses and for their disobedience John Daunt, Robert Tanner and John Draycote were outlawed in the same month. That October, as King's Bench convened for Michaelmas Term, Agnes's hopes of getting justice may have been raised by the news that four of the accused, Nicholas Jones, David Jones, Thomas Tanner and Thomas Halyday, would appear in court. The following month they did stand before the bench. However, they came not to plead, but to flaunt pardons they had bought from the king, and which rendered them immune from further prosecution for their activities at Nibley Green. The remaining accused, Daunt, Robert Tanner and Draycote, were summoned once more, and once more the summonses were ignored. There is no record of a successful prosecution of any of John Lewis's alleged murderers. Such a course of events is far from unique, and may reflect nothing more than the imperfections of the fifteenth-century justice system. On the other hand, Agnes may have been included in the settlement made between Berkeley and Margaret Talbot, and dropped her suit in return for some kind of compensation, but it is at least possible that after Edward IV's restoration Agnes's association with the discredited Lord Berkeley made her task much more difficult, and ultimately impossible.

4

RESOLUTION

The seal was put on William, Lord Berkeley's rehabilitation in April 1475, when his five-year-old son, Thomas, was made a Knight of the Bath at the creation of Edward as prince of Wales.[1] On this occasion, as he approached his fiftieth year, once more enjoying royal favour, with his old enemies vanquished and his titles secured, William could have been forgiven for looking forward to a tranquil and prosperous old age. But this was most certainly not to be. His remaining seventeen years would see him not only fighting the next generation of claimants to the entailed lands, but also bitterly at odds with his own brother. The seed of this new round of conflict had been sown just one month earlier.

On 14 March 1475 Sir Edward Grey, husband of Elizabeth, sole surviving sister and heiress to Thomas Talbot, Viscount Lisle, was created Lord Lisle.[2] By now, Grey and Berkeley had probably already locked horns over the disputed property. In the words of John Smyth,

> Between these two, this Sir Edward Grey, and this lord William, was longe tossed with equall malice and greatness the title of these manors and lands, like a ball of discord, taken up and banded, with much toyle and expence.[3]

We do not know which side first lofted this 'ball of discord', but the Berkeleys were certainly pursuing their new enemies through the courts by the end of 1475, when John Wenlock esquire of London petitioned the court of Chancery. His complaint was that Lord Berkeley and his brothers Maurice and Thomas had been prosecuting vexatious suits against him in the courts of Common Pleas and King's Bench. The Berkeleys were claiming that Wenlock, as a former servant in the Talbot household at Wotton-under-Edge, had been implicated in the events of 1451 when the brothers had been captured by the earl of Shrewsbury's men.[4] But the real motive behind these suits, Wenlock claimed, was to put pressure on him to release certain deeds and other evidences he held on behalf of Lord and Lady Lisle and their associates. Without doubt, these documents related to the disputed properties, and had perhaps been saved from the Berkeleys' seizure of the Wotton muniments on the day of Nibley Green. Quite possibly, they included the indentures which the Berkeleys had signed under duress in 1451, by which they were bound not to contest the Talbots' right to the disputed properties. These bonds had never been cancelled, and had obviously been flouted on many occasions; in the right circumstances they could have been a decisive weapon in Lisle's armoury.

In February 1482 an attempt was made to settle the dispute through the mediation of Thomas Grey, marquis of Dorset, Queen Elizabeth Woodville's son, Lord Lisle's nephew, and friend of the Berkeleys. Lisle and Berkeley agreed that the latter should retain the disputed properties (but they would remain to Lord and Lady Lisle and their heirs after the death of Viscount Berkeley, as William was now titled) and in return pay an annuity to the Lisles. This was to be £20 while the annuity of £100 was still being paid to Margaret Talbot, according to the Act of 1472, but would increase to £100 thereafter. The settlement did not last three months, and in May the royal Council bound Berkeley in £1,000 not to harm Lisle or his servants.[5] At some point between 1483 and 1487 Lord Lisle took Berkeley – now earl of Nottingham – to Chancery, complaining that he had not honoured the agreement of 1482, and demanding the return of documents relating to the settlement.[6]

William Berkeley's spectacular rise through the ranks of the peerage – he would end his days as marquis of Berkeley – was, in its origins, connected with the spectre of the £34,000 to which the 1451 indentures rendered him liable. In the spring of 1476 Lord Berkeley's two children, Thomas and Katherine, died, aged six and two respectively. William was fifty, and the chances of his fathering any more children looked slim indeed. He seems to have resigned himself to the probability of dying childless, and resolved to make the best of this situation.

His opportunity had been presented by the death of John Mowbray, duke of Norfolk, in January 1476.[7] He left one child, Anne, born in 1473. This three-year-old was now the greatest heiress in England. Edward IV wasted little time in snapping her up for his infant younger son Richard, duke of York, and the two children were married in January 1478. At the same time, parliament decreed that should Anne die without heirs of her body her inheritance would remain with Duke Richard for the rest of his life and not, as was customary, return to her next heirs. Her next heirs were John, Lord Howard, and William, Lord Berkeley. These two shared the same grandparents, Thomas Mowbray, earl of Norfolk and Elizabeth, daughter of Richard, earl of Arundel; and their uncle, John, duke of Norfolk, was Anne's great-grandfather. While Edward IV was prepared to ride roughshod over other people's property claims when it suited him, on this occasion he preferred to negotiate. Anne's mother, Elizabeth, dowager duchess of Norfolk, was happy to accede to this plan, since she was a daughter of John, first earl of Shrewsbury, and saw it as a means of disinheriting her family's enemy, Lord Berkeley. Edward persuaded Berkeley and Howard to surrender their reversionary interests in the Mowbray inheritance. If the duke of York died without heirs of his body, the property would remain to the king and his heirs male; only if the king died without a surviving male heir would the inheritance descend to Berkeley and Howard or their heirs. In return, the king promised to pay off Berkeley's obligation to the Talbots, now valued at £34,000.[8] Edward probably had no intention of actually doing so, but with this commitment from the king, any attempt by the Talbots' heirs to use the indentures against Berkeley would have been virtually impossible; just in case, the king undertook to give Berkeley the documents containing the bonds and obligations, and to guarantee him and his brothers immunity from prosecution on the basis of the 1451 agreements. He was also admitted to the royal Council and granted a councillor's 100-mark annuity. As a further inducement for the surrender of his reversionary interest, Lord William was to be created Viscount Berkeley.

At his creation on 21 April 1481 at Greenwich Palace, wearing the robes of a viscount, standing before the king as the letters patent recording his creation were recited, did Berkeley recall other letters, written a decade before: 'Thomas Talbot, otherwise called viscont Lisle, not long continued in that name but a new found thing brought out of Strange Contryes'? That this title was still something of a 'new found thing' in 1481 would have been impressed upon him shortly before this ceremony, when the heralds had to admit that they did not know what robes should be worn by a viscount, so rare and unfamiliar was the rank. One of them was despatched to the earl of Essex, who had once held the title of Viscount Bourchier, to ask his opinion, but his answer did not satisfy all of the heralds. Eventually, they settled for an earl's robes, with fewer fur trimmings.[9] Did the new Viscount Berkeley savour the irony of the situation?

This was a very good deal for Berkeley. He had surrendered rights which he would not have enjoyed anyway had Anne Mowbray produced children.

Without children of his own, he probably felt that he had a free hand to bargain away such distant prospects for immediate gain. What he had gained was royal protection from his Talbot-Grey enemies – it is no wonder that he would feel little compulsion to abide by the February 1482 agreement with Lord Lisle – and a new and grander title.

In fact, the deal turned out to be far better than Berkeley could possibly have hoped at its making. Seven months after Viscount Berkeley's creation, Anne Mowbray died. This brought him a little closer to his share of the Mowbray inheritance, but Edward quickly secured the transmission of the property to the duke of York. The viscount's pulse surely did not race at the news of young Anne's death. But another death, and the removal from the scene of two more children, presented an extraordinary opportunity for the viscount. Edward IV died on 9 April 1483. The following month his brother, Richard, duke of Gloucester, had declared his nephews illegitimate and seized the throne as Richard III. Edward V and Richard, duke of York disappeared into the Tower and were never seen again. This still did not mean that the Mowbray inheritance would fall into Berkeley's hands: it had been conferred on York by an Act of Parliament, and only another Act could legally deprive him of lands or titles, despite his supposed bastardy. Also, despite the fact that he was probably murdered in the Tower by order of Richard III, he would never officially be declared dead, with the consequence that his Mowbray lands could not legally descend to his next heir, who in any case would be the king. Nothing daunted, and calculating that Richard the usurper desperately needed supporters in the south, Berkeley petitioned the king for his share of the inheritance. His petition was granted a mere two days after Richard's accession. John Howard also received his share of the Mowbray lands, and in fact it is likely that the alacrity with which Richard acceded to these arrangements was prompted mainly by his desire to win Howard's support, since he could raise more men than Berkeley, and was the key to controlling East Anglia. Richard could hardly make the concession to Howard without an equal offer to Berkeley. Along with lands came titles: on 28 June Howard became duke of Norfolk, and Berkeley was created earl of Nottingham, one of the lesser titles that accompanied the Mowbray inheritance. There was no legal justification for any of this.

While one might admire Berkeley's dynamism, imagination and sheer effrontery – assuming that the initiative came from him and not from Howard – this episode also emphasises the more sinister side to his character. He would have been drafting his petition before Richard's seizure of power, while Edward V and his young brother were still at liberty, and by its success he must surely have known that the boys would never be allowed their freedom. Perhaps he also realised that these arrangements signalled their imminent demise. We can never know if he felt any qualms of conscience as he received his earldom and the equivalent of over eighty-six manors and lordships, with other lands, in twelve English counties, Wales and Ireland.

Now, as John Smyth noted, Earl William could have 'soared in height of honor and greatness of Estate above the heads of all his Ancestors'.[10] Instead, he embarked upon an extraordinary policy of trading lands for cash and title. In March 1484 he agreed to grant thirty-five of his Mowbray manors to Richard III and the heirs of his body in return for an annuity of 400 marks from the London customs and the promise of Richard's good lordship. Since the dispute with Lord Lisle was still rumbling on – Berkeley was at that point bound in £1,000 to appear before the Council and to desist from attacking Lisle or his servants – it is likely that this deal was designed to give the earl further leverage in the courts, and perhaps to provide him with ready cash to pay his legal fees. Two general pardons to Berkeley, granted in April and December 1484, may also have been part of the deal.[11] Joan had died the month before William's grant of the Mowbray manors, and it may be that his wife's death removed any lingering hopes of an heir, while also reminding him of his own mortality, and so prompted this radical action. The manors Berkeley had granted to Richard were to return to him if the king died without heirs of his body. The decease of Richard's wife and only child, and then his own death at Bosworth in August 1485, meant that these thirty-five manors came back into Berkeley's hands. Once again astonishing good fortune had vindicated his judgement. Smyth, as one would expect, saw it in providential terms:

> Soe willing was Gods gracious eye to have made this Earle looke back, and to retire himself into the consideration of himselfe, and to have preserved those possessions which had been from heaven showred upon him.[12]

Earl William's role in the Bosworth campaign is obscure – he seems to have followed the Stanleys' example and avoided commitment to either side until he could be reasonably sure of the outcome – but he seems to have learnt from his mistakes in 1471 and, as Smyth grudgingly admits,

> soe prudent was this Earles cariage between those adverse princes and their adherents, (ayding the one with men, the other with money,

neither of both with his person,) That hee preserved the favor of both, at least lost neither of them.[13]

Earl William officiated at Henry VII's coronation and was created earl marshal and great marshal of England, with a £20 annuity, in February 1486.[14] For this honour he had to thank the influence of his long-standing associate Sir William Stanley, now the king's lord chamberlain. But Stanley's assistance did not come cheap, whatever friendship may have existed between them. On the same day as his creation as marshal, William granted to Stanley and to the heirs of his body two Welsh castles and his own share in twenty-eight manors.

Seen in the context of his dispute with Lisle, his conduct up to this point, if at times rash, nonetheless seems to have had the perfectly rational aim of securing royal protection from his enemies. From 1486 however, it appears that rationality is eclipsed by two overwhelming obsessions. The first might be guessed from his career so far: the desire for further aggrandisement. Having climbed from mere baron to earl in a little over two years, and with ample resources behind him, why not go further? Marquisates and dukedoms beckoned. He had already shown a willingness to sacrifice some part of his landed estate to this end. Old and childless as he was, he evidently saw little reason to favour his posterity at the expense of his present gratification. But while childless he was not, of course, lacking an heir. Since 1476 Maurice had stood to inherit his brother's increasingly impressive estate; after the death of his younger brother Thomas in July 1484, he was the sole heir. He now looked on with growing anxiety as his patrimony, and that of his four children, was put at risk in William's quest for titles. According to Leland, Maurice 'solde and dyd bargen for his owne Sunne', that is, his eldest son, also called Maurice, to be recognised as 'Heire apparent to the Landes'. The earl was enraged by such pressure. According to Smyth, 'great displeasures now arose, never after reconciled' between him and his brother and nephew. Earl William accused his brother of having disparaged his family by his marriage to Isabel, daughter of a Bristol merchant. Smyth took great offence at this accusation:

How little cause the Marques Berkeley had to complaine of the obscure parentage of the lady Isable, which he vainly called base: and of the unworthynes of his brothers match with so mean bloud, as hee reproached it, making that a motive to his own vast expences, and of the disinheritance of this lord his brother, least any of her base bloud should

100

inherite after him, may to his further reproof bee returned upon his memory to bee but a fained and unbrotherly quarrell picked on purpose to give colour for his own exorbitances: Like vaine were his exceptions to his said brother and heire, for defending the vertue of his wife and worthiness of her parentage.[15]

Indeed, there is no evidence that prior to this altercation William had objected to the marriage, which had taken place as long ago as 1465. The two brothers appear to have been on good terms until at least 1484, and their falling out may date to no earlier than 1486, when the Stanley grant was made.[16] This grant might well have prompted Maurice to confront his brother. This was also the year in which William married his third and final wife, Anne, daughter of Thomas Fiennes, Lord Dacre of the South. Smyth had little time for Anne Fiennes:

> This lady Anne wrought profitably upon the age of her old husband both for the advancement of her self and of her kindred; And, if not the raiser yet certainly a continuer of the storme that blew soe unnat-urall a vapour between her husband and Maurice his brother and heire.

William's second obsession, in short, was the ruination of his own brother.

Leland's account of William's vengeance on his brother puts it in a nutshell: 'Lord Berkeley in a Rage made King Henry the 7 his Heire for moste of his Lands, and after was made a Marquise...'.[17] The process began in the winter of 1487, when Earl William settled the castle and manor of Berkeley and five other manors on himself and the heirs of his body, with remainder to Henry VII and his male heirs. Four other manors were settled on himself and his wife, with the same condition. There was no possibility of William and Anne producing children, so in effect this settlement ensured that after their deaths these properties would go not to Maurice, but to the king. In return, in January 1489, William received the title of marquis of Berkeley. Further settlements followed, with William receiving annuities in return.[18] Apart from the king, the major beneficiaries of William's liquida-tion of his patrimony were his old associates Thomas Stanley, earl of Derby, the king's father-in-law, and his younger brother Sir William Stanley, together with Sir Reginald Bray, Henry VII's leading financial administrator, and the family of Robert, Lord Willoughby, steward of the royal household, to whom William was related through his second wife.[19] If William hoped that the recipients would use their influence with the king to get him a dukedom, he would be disappointed. He died a marquis, having promised away nearly all his landed wealth, including the very properties for whose possession men had died, and he and his brothers had fought and been prepared to kill. Not for nothing did Smyth call the marquis of Berkeley 'William the wast all'.

This is no ordinary story of an eccentric in his rancorous old age. There is something pathological about William's behaviour in his later years. Smyth may seem too quick to blame Anne Fiennes for his sudden and terrible anger: Lady Macbeth, who first appeared on stage thirteen years before Smyth completed his *Lives*, reminds us that the manipulative wife corrupting a weak husband is an all-too-common gender stereotype. There is nonetheless a striking coincidence between William's third marriage and the onset of conflict with his brother. If Anne was taking advantage of a mentally unstable husband – and one does wonder how, exactly, she sought to benefit from his actions – then she was not alone. From Henry VII downwards, the recipients of William's largesse appear to have been perfectly willing to benefit from his foolishness, and there is no indication that any of his intended beneficiaries declined his offers.

There was one more folly to be committed by William and his wife before their deaths. In the summer of 1490 William contracted stonemasons and carpenters to begin building a grand new dwelling on his manor of Great Chesterford in Essex, which he had already pledged to Henry VII. Smyth cannot contain his exasperation at this act:

> As though it was not enough to give the king his land, but hee would build him an house also;... At which time, without a like miraculous blessing as was sent to Abraham and Sara, there was noe hope of issue between him and his wife, And himself before the finishing could not but fall into his grave, as he did...[20]

His spiritual well-being was the other project about which the marquis busied himself in his declining years. In 1488 and 1489 he gave bequests to Wallingwells Priory in Nottinghamshire and to Worcester Cathedral, in return for prayers to be said for himself, his wives Anne and Joan, Anne's father, his children by Joan, and Thomas Stanley, earl of Derby.[21] He was also making arrangements for his death and burial. He chose as his resting place the Augustinian Friary in London's Broad Street, where his wife Joan lay buried. That the Berkeley mausoleum was now to be in London rather than Berkeley or Bristol is an indication of the family's expanded horizons, and pretensions, perhaps. In November 1490 he promised £100 and other gifts to the friary in return for prayers for himself and Anne, Joan and her Willoughby and Mowbray relatives, for his parents and for his brother Thomas; Maurice, father and son, were of course missing from this litany. In his will, made on 5 February 1492, he asked to be buried at the friary, to which he bequeathed a total of 220 marks.[22] He left many other bequests, providing prayers, establishing a chantry in Lincolnshire, purchasing a papal remission of sin for those who prayed for his soul, and giving Anne one half of his plate and household goods. He willed that his executors,

> after my deciese satisfie and Recompense all trespasis and wronges by me doon and not recompensed afore my deccese in discharge of my soule suche as shalbe shewne and provided before them within x yeris next after my deceese And that to be proclamid in every place where I have had most resort unto in tymes past to thentent my dettes and the seid wrongis may be truely content and satisfied after every true and resonable mannes desire.

A labour, one might think, of Herculean proportions. He gave money to distant Berkeley relatives, to servants, and could even find twenty shillings for his cook, but of his brother and nephew there is not a word. William died on St Valentine's night 1492, and was given a sumptuous funeral.[23] To his brother he left nothing but debts. Smyth recounts how, after Berkeley's death, Maurice was sued by William Moore, former secretary to the marquis who, he claimed, had promised him on his death bed repayment of a loan of £10 7s in unpaid wages. Maurice paid him,

> though hee was neither heire nor Executor, and not having any Assets in land or personall estate from his said brother; whereby appeares a great distance between the disposition of these two brothers; The Marques hatinge Maurice at his death, Maurice lovinge his memory and the repose of his soule after life ended.

Soon after William's death Henry VII took possession of Berkeley Castle and spent ten days there with his queen. In preparation for his visit, Anne had the hall at Wotton House demolished, and used the lead from its roof to refurbish the castle kitchen, whereby that prime mansion seat of Wotton became wholly devastated; which for the space of 280 years had been as a Queen of houses to this noble family; having thereby nothing left her but ruins and those ill witnesses of her perished beauty, declaring thereby that houses as well as men have their ages and destines.[24]

Viewing the wreck of his inheritance Maurice, the new Lord Berkeley, left with only his estate at Thornbury and in his fifty-seventh year, might have been forgiven for concluding that his destiny was to end his days in relative poverty. But this was not a fate he was willing to accept. Instead, this remarkable man spent the remaining fourteen years of his life trying to recover what his brother had thrown away. By his death in 1506, he had successfully reclaimed around fifty manors. Smyth's depiction of 'Maurice the Lawier' about this business is irresistible:

> with a milk-white head in his irksome old age of 70 years, in winter terms and frosty seasons, with a buckram bagg stuffed with law cases, in early mornings and late evenings walking with his eldest son between the four Inns of Court and Westminster Hall, following his law suits in his own person, not for himself, but for his posterity, to regaine part of those possessions wich a vast brother had profusely consumed.[25]

These restored estates passed down through three further generations of Berkeley lords.[26] In 1553 Maurice's great-grandson, Henry, 17th Lord Berkeley, recovered the castle and lordship of Berkeley by the death without issue of Edward VI. But the king's death brought in its train both triumph and potential disaster for the Berkeleys. Later in the same year John Dudley, duke of Northumberland, was attainted and executed for his part in the failed attempt to put Lady Jane Grey on the throne. Northumberland was the grandson and heir of Edward Grey, Lord Lisle. By his attainder his Lisle inheritance was forfeited to the crown; along with it came the Lisle claim to the disputed Berkeley properties. Queen Mary and then Elizabeth made desultory attempts to pursue the Lisle claim, but it was only after 1572, when the Berkeleys offended Robert Dudley, earl of Leicester (Northumberland's son) by their refusal of an offer of a marriage alliance, that it became a serious threat. The following year, with the queen's encouragement, Leicester secured a verdict against Lord Berkeley. He was ordered to surrender the manors of Simondshall and Wotton and to pay more than £5,000 to the crown. There were further losses in 1580. Together, Berkeley lost nearly half his manors to the queen, who as soon as she got them granted them to the Dudleys. In addition, he had to sell his Wiltshire, Warwickshire, Leicestershire and Norfolk estates to pay the massive fines, damages and legal expenses incurred. Maurice Lord Berkeley's hard-won legacy was being consumed at an alarming rate. At last, in 1609, the Lisles and the Berkeleys reached a final settlement: the Berkeleys were to keep the disputed Lisle properties, but in return were to pay Sir Robert Sidney, the current Lord Lisle, £7,320 to discharge all claims. John Smyth was himself involved in the legal manoeuvres that led up to the settlement. After 192 years, the great Berkeley law suit had come to an end.

5

The Myth of Nibley Green

Smyth began writing his great history even before the Berkeley dispute was finally settled. His work – combined with the terse accounts of Leland and Camden, and seasoned with varying degrees of speculation and invention – provided the basis for a number of eighteenth- and nineteenth-century treatments of the battle of Nibley Green and its immediate context. These have created what might be described as 'The Myth of Nibley Green'. The two pioneering county histories of Gloucestershire, Atkyns' *The Ancient and Present State of Gloucestershire*, published in 1711, and Rudder's *A New History of Gloucestershire* of 1779 both give a brief, fairly neutral account of the battle and its causes, derived from Smyth.[1] Both give the figures of 1,000 combatants in total with 150 casualties resulting from the fray. Smyth simply stated that Lord Berkeley had about 1,000 men, and that his army exceeded that of Lisle's, with no mention of the number of casualties. There is no apparent basis in fact for the figure of 150 casualties: Rudder seems simply to have followed Atkyns, but how Atkyns came by this figure is not known. Certainly, no reference to such numbers has been found in contemporary sources.[2]

While the *Lives of the Berkeleys* was used in manuscript by local historians and antiquarians, it was not until the publication in 1821 of Thomas Fosbrooke's *Berkeley Manuscripts: Abstracts and Extracts of Smyth's Lives of the Berkeleys*, that any part of Smyth's work became widely available. Fosbrooke displays a touchingly naïve belief in the total accuracy of Smyth's writing, confidently stating, 'as the whole Work is compiled from Records and Original Papers, the authenticity is indisputable'. For him, one of the most important aspects of the work was its highly detailed record of Berkeley legal proceedings, which presented 'an insight into the Constitution, which has rarely, if ever, been preconceived, at most by Lawyers and Antiquaries only'.[3]

Fosbrooke's publication appeared two years after Sir Walter Scott's *Ivanhoe*, and two years before his *Quentin Durward*. Both novels were set in the Middle Ages. Scott may be said to have invented the historical novel, or at least, the

To the R.t Hon.ble the Countess of Berkley this View
of Berkley Castle in Gloucestershire copied from a Drawing of her Ladyships is most humbly dedicated.

32. An eighteenth-century view of Berkeley Castle.

novel with aspirations to being grounded in historical reality: before him, Gothic novelists and poets had delighted in a make-believe Middle Ages of mad monks and haunted castles; after Scott, novelists had to make some nod in the direction of historical veracity. Scott was both novelist and historian, and combined these roles brilliantly. Most of those who came after him were less gifted.

The dramatic events of the Berkeley-Lisle feud are in many ways a gift for the historical novelist, and they soon found their interpreter. Alas, it was not Scott. What he would have made of the tale we can only imagine. Instead, it was a man who, as a member of the Berkeley family, doubtless felt himself admirably qualified for the job. Others did not share his confidence. What resulted from his efforts, and their reception, was one of the most remarkable episodes in the development of the Nibley Green myth, and indeed, a fascinating chapter of Berkeley family history in its own right. In 1836, four years after Scott's death – thereby allowing him, perhaps, to spin in his grave – Grantley Berkeley, the sixth son of Frederick Augustus, Lord Berkeley, produced a three-volume novel entitled, *Berkeley Castle: An Historical Romance*, a love story, interwoven with the events surrounding the battle of Nibley Green.[4] In his introduction Berkeley states his intention to impose a believable love story upon a real episode in his family's history, stating grandly, 'I shall say nothing of import, unless fully borne out by ancient reference'. His 'ancient reference' is Smyth's manuscript, which Berkeley proudly states is laid before him as he writes. However, his is very far from being a historically accurate version of events.

All of the characters mentioned by Smyth in his account of the battle, whether hesitatingly or not, are thrown into the fray and blended with several original creations. There is little reason to suppose that Berkeley's version of the chain of events preceding the battle is anything more than an artistic invention. The story is narrated by an invented hero, Herbert Reardon, an esquire of Sir Maurice Berkeley. At one stage in the novel he is sent to spy on the plotters Thomas Holt and Robert Vele as they plan to take Berkeley Castle by subterfuge. Reardon chases Vele but unfortunately Lisle's tenant is the 'fastest man in England' and escapes. Rufus Mull, the brother of one of Lisle's real-life retainers, Thomas Mull, is, bizarrely, plotting a forced marriage to Isabel, the daughter of Philip Mede, the Bristol merchant. In the closing stages of the battle of Nibley Green Sir Maurice and Reardon manage to drag themselves away from slaughtering Lisle's routed forces in order to arrive at the church in time to stop the marriage ceremony; they kill Rufus Mull, thus saving Isabel from a life of torment. Black Will appears as a 'surly retainer' of Lord Berkeley, famous for assaulting a River Severn harbour master. His, now infamous, archery skills are introduced to Lord Berkeley just before the battle: 'Your Lordship has several foresters here among your archers, one a shrewd

33. The interior of St Mary's Church, Berkeley, where, according to Grantley Berkeley, Isabel Mede was saved from a forced marriage to Thomas Mull.

fellow, commonly known by the name of Black Will'. His other identity, also lifted straight from the pages of Smyth, as William Long, son of Thomas Long, is revealed later in the story.

According to Berkeley, before the battle Thomas, the youngest surviving Berkeley son, was sent to raise the men of Bristol, Shipward was to recruit the men of Redcliff and then Thornbury and there he was to meet with Hilp and proceed to 'Druid's Oak' on the outskirts of the wood, by seven the following morning. All of these names are familiar from the pages of Smyth: they were named either by Margaret Talbot in the court case brought against the Berkeleys and their retainers, or from the case brought by Shipward and Mede against those who slanderously accused them of involvement in the battle. James Hyett, steward of St Briavels, receives a mention but is not a figure of importance: Grantley Berkeley obviously saw his name in Smyth, but did not know of Hyett's true significance. Among the important characters for whom there is no historical record, Sir Andrew Johnston, a key Berkeley retainer and guest at the castle, leads the 'heavy infantry'. George Wyrall leads the archers drawn from the Forest of Dean, and is described thus: 'with the exception of your Lordship, [he] is supposed to have more power in the forest than anyone else'.

Grantley Berkeley's vivid description of the battle is certainly the most detailed we have, but unfortunately, it seems to be far more the product of imagination than historical research. From the detail that Berkeley gives it is clear that he had visited the battle site, which his family owned. His account of how the topography may have influenced the course of the battle deserves serious consideration, but the landscape in which his characters fight is that of the nineteenth century, not the fifteenth, and little account is taken of how it may have changed in the interim. The dark, sunken lane that runs east up the hill from the battle site to the church suggests that a fleeing force could have been trapped and perhaps slaughtered there. In his story this is exactly what happens. The broken Lisle force breaks into three groups, fleeing around either side of the hill to their rear, and along the sunken lane that runs up the hill. The huge old oak tree in front of Bush Street Farm, massive even in 1836, seems to have been chosen by Berkeley as the Druid's Oak, the landmark where his ancestor mustered his men on the edge of Michaelwood Chase before battle was joined. However, this tree would have been far smaller in 1470 and would have been merely one tree among many in the woods that stretched down to the Swynebourne Stream. In turn this tiny stream, scarcely noticeable today, and just as insignificant on the nineteenth-century ordnance survey maps, could be portrayed as a major obstacle, a marshy strip that was an impediment to the 400 horse that Berkeley apparently divided between his flanks!

Berkeley's description of the fighting itself is even more inventive: for the purposes of the novelist, of course, it has to be, since Smyth records so little information on the subject. Smyth's statement that there were about 1,000 men on Lord Berkeley's side is elaborated to include 'four hundred horse, and six hundred infantry, three hundred of whom were archers'. The preliminaries to the battle are described in great detail with Lisle drawn up on the hill opposite at an angle to Berkeley's force, which is hidden in the trees across the green:

> By this time Lord Lisle appeared to be aware of our presence, for there was an evident bustle along the left of his line next us. Our position was very strong: in front, and separating the Chase from the green, was some broken and swampy ground, caused by a sort of water-course, called Fowlshard; over which, though passable anywhere by infantry, there were only two places by which cavalry could reach the field, and opposite to these our bodies of horse were placed in readiness to act at a moment's notice. The wood was in our rear, and the whole sidelong slope of the common or green directly in front; the left of Lord Lisle's line forming an angle with our right. Placed thus, the strength of the enemy's position was obvious, as our folly would have been had we advanced up the hill in the face of it; and, besides this, it was none of our leader's plan either to make the first assault or throw an advantage carelessly away.

In the story it is Lord Berkeley himself who provokes the fatal downhill assault by Lord Lisle:

> Lord Berkeley – sheathed from head to foot in black and burnished iron inlaid with gold, mounted on his stately white war-horse, with his long lance poised on high, his heavy battle-axe at his saddle-bow, and his shield suspended round his neck, his lofty crimson plume waving in the light air – advanced about ten yards on the open green, preceded by his trumpets and banner and halted in full sight of the enemy. The trumpets of the foe replied to the flourish of ours, and the leaders of the opposing parties continued gazing upon each other for some moments; Lord Berkeley and his well-broken steed as stationary and motionless as if they had been hewn from a rock of marble.
>   A little bustle soon began to be distinguishable in the enemy's right; and, presently after, his whole line wheeled upon its left, bringing its front directly opposite ours, and occupying the whole slope of the green

crosswise… Word was given for an advance of their whole line, their archers being thrown forward with their arrows drawn.

Lord Berkeley returns to head the right flank of cavalry while Lisle continues to advance. When Lisle's host proceeds to within fifty yards of the gorse on the edge of the wood Wryall orders his archers to stand and unleash a devastating volley. The charge is sounded and Lord Berkeley leads his horse straight at Lisle's position with his entire army close behind:

> For a space it was impossible to know how matters were going; arrows continued to fly at intervals, mingled with the shouts for Berkeley and Lisle and the clash of weapons; and several times I was conscious of trampling over the dead and dying. At this moment, a loud cry arose, which made itself heard above the surrounding confusion, that 'Lisle was down'.

Lisle's army turns to flee in three directions with Berkeley's men in pursuit. Only after the rescue of Isabel does Grantley Berkeley return to Smyth's work to describe the sacking of Wotton House. Far from pursuing Lady Lisle around the neighbouring villages, however, in the story Lord Berkeley is perfectly chivalrous:

> Everything that came in the way was broken to pieces by our infuriated followers, or flung out of the windows. They were continuing their excesses, when, on one of the landing-places of the principal staircase, a lady appeared in an agony of distress, and conjured Lord Berkeley to pause, and order his vassals to quit the house, for Lady Lisle was taken ill, and, from her delicate situation, the loss of her life might be the consequence.

What makes Grantley Berkeley's novel of more interest, and gives it a place in the history of his family, are the events that resulted from a venomous review written by William Maginn, and which appeared in *Fraser's Magazine* in August 1836.[5] Two substantial accounts of the affair are extant. The first is contained in the January 1837 edition of the magazine, and provides a verbatim transcription of proceedings in the Exchequer Court.[6] The second is a later memoir by Grantley Berkeley, *My Life and Recollections*, in which his version of events is given in great detail.[7]

According to Berkeley the story began when he was mysteriously accosted in the street by a member of London's literary society whom he gallantly refers

34. Grantley Berkeley, from the frontispiece to his *My Life and Recollections*, vol. 1 (1865).

to only as Miss _____. Berkeley's description of their first meeting is as flowery as the love story in his novel:

> Never shall I forget the look she gave me. Her lips became compressed over her beautiful teeth (the eyes and teeth were the attractions of her face), and in that one glance from beneath those delicate eyelashes, I read the soul within – the terrible reality of her life, not 'the poetry of it' – and knew that at that moment the light in her eyes was softened, almost subdued by a tear of anguish.

A subsequent meeting followed when Berkeley discovered the cause of Miss _____'s sorrow, namely, the machinations of William Maginn, 'an Irishman of considerable talent' but whose 'constant pressure of debt and drunkenness had prevented his producing any substantive work'. Miss _____ was a budding writer. Maginn had exaggerated his influence as an editor and critic to attempt to 'obtain power over her for personal seduction'. The fact that the young lady's mother also relied on her publishing work only increased Maginn's hold over her. Grantley Berkeley immediately set about discovering exactly who this Maginn was and soon reached the conclusion that he was, in reality, 'a literary adventurer who lived a hand-to-mouth existence on what he gained by writing for newspapers and magazines, was as often in prison as out, and much more frequently drunk than sober'. Miss _____ was advised to refuse to admit Maginn to her home again and was to sever all ties with him, and any referral was to be addressed to Berkeley, whose chestnut mare was to be seen very frequently outside her house. Berkeley was warned that Maginn was aware of his interference and was biding his time before seeking revenge. Therefore, if Berkeley's account can be believed, Maginn's savage review owed more to a personal vendetta than to aesthetic appreciation of the novel.

Maginn's review was truly scathing, of both the work and its author. Berkeley recalls that the novel was generally received 'indulgently' except for the article by Maginn which, 'in the guise of a review of my book, was a most offensive and personal attack on me'. As a Member of Parliament and prominent London society figure Grantley Berkeley was something of a target even before he embarked upon this literary endeavour. The review begins with a general attack on the closed ranks of gentlemen in London society who sneer from their pedestal of exclusivity at those below them. Their talk is of 'horses, and carriages, and operas, and parks and the last parties'. However, according to Maginn, when one of these gentlemen steps away from this

charmed circle he often proves himself to be something of a 'blockhead', a
state of affairs which is compounded by literary pretensions:

> When he takes a pen in his hand, he not only displays a dire ignorance
> and stupidity, but, in nine cases out of ten, an utter meanness of thought
> and manners, and a crawling vulgarity of soul… If nature had bestowed
> upon them brains – a fact very much open to dispute – those brains are
> always wasted by the frivolities in which they constantly engage, and the
> silly talk which forms the staple of their existence.

This diatribe continues for a page and a half before turning to Grantley
Berkeley and his family. Maginn immediately seizes upon what was an acutely
embarrassing fact for the Berkeley family:

> Why… is his eldest brother pitch-forked into the house of Lords by the
> title of Lord Segrave? Why does he not sit there as earl of Berkeley?…
> Mr Grantley Berkeley's mother lived with Mr Grantley Berkeley's father
> as his mistress, and… she had at least one child before she could induce
> the old and very stupid lord to marry her. All this is set down in the
> journals of the House of Lords. Why, then under such circumstances,
> bore us with long panegyrics upon the purity, antiquity and nobility of
> the Berkeley blood? Why torment us with a book vilely written,
> without any other end, object or aim, but to prove that the Lord of
> Berkeley was a great man once upon a time?

Maginn had hit upon a subject that had cast a shadow over the Berkeley family
for decades. Frederick Augustus, Lord Berkeley, had apparently married Mary
Cole in a private ceremony at Lambeth on 30 March 1785. They chose to
keep this a secret and did not openly marry at Berkeley until 16 May 1796,
Lady Berkeley being known as Miss Tudor for the entire eleven-year period
between the two ceremonies.[8] During this time Mary gave birth to four sons.
Other sons followed after the second ceremony, of whom the first was
Thomas Moreton Fitzhardinge, followed by Grantley and then his youngest
brother, Craven. On his death in 1810 the old lord left everything to his eldest
son William, who had already attempted to establish his right to inherit the
earldom of Berkeley before the House of Lords. As early as 1799 William had
obtained permission to lay his pedigree before the Lords and in 1801 he made
a full deposition to the House about the marriage ceremonies. Despite these
efforts, William was refused the earldom of Berkeley on the grounds that the

existence of his parents' first marriage had not been established. Now, having inherited Berkeley Castle, William tried to claim a writ of summons to the Lords as a baron, arguing that the barony passed automatically to the owner of the castle. The committee of privileges, in trying to decide the issue, even went to the lengths of dragging up documents relating to the 1349 entail that had led to the original feud between the heirs male, and heirs general, although the entail was considered no longer relevant. The committee came to no firm conclusion.[9] William continued to be known by his military rank, as Colonel Berkeley, until being created Baron Segrave of Berkeley in 1831 and, finally, Earl Fitzhardinge in 1841. The Fitzhardinge title was inherited from brother to brother until it reached Thomas, the fifth son, and first to be able to claim the full title, but he refused to do so as a point of principle. Grantley, as the sixth son, remained heir to his childless brother for nearly seventy years until his death in 1881. It was Grantley's support for his eldest brother that had led to a concerted family plan to become Members of Parliament. Grantley himself sat for West Gloucestershire from 1832 to 1852 while his younger brother Craven sat for Cheltenham from 1832 to 1865. By attacking the proud Berkeley pedigree Maginn was launching a personal attack, beyond a simple book review.

Following a description of Berkeley's maternal grandfather as a Gloucestershire butcher we finally, on the third page of a $5\frac{1}{2}$-page book review, get to a critique of the novel itself. Maginn describes the backdrop to the novel, the Wars of the Roses, as a period when, 'the Berkeleys were distinguished only for carrying on a lawsuit among themselves; and skulking like cowards, from the field, to appear as beggars before whatever faction ruled the court.' Maginn's appreciation of the novel itself is predictably forthright: 'As for the book, it is trash. There is not the shadow of a story in it'. Much of the final two pages is composed of the quotation and dissection of sections of the novel in detail before finishing with a flourish: 'Berkeley Castle in conception is the most impertinent, as in execution it is about the stupidest it has ever been our misfortune to read'.

The August edition of Fraser's Magazine, which contained the review, came out on the first of the month and Grantley seems to have been forwarded a copy by Colonel Berkeley immediately, for in his Recollections he admits that he went to see the editor of Fraser's some days later, and we know that this visit was on 3 August. Berkeley, who presents himself as something of an heroic man of action, decided that this insulting attack was one example of a larger problem whereby a portion of the press felt at liberty to abuse its privileges by attacking prominent figures. Flouting the spirit of the libel laws, which protected the identity of writers and placed no pressure on their editors, Berkeley decided to take matters into his own hands and immediately set off for London.

Berkeley's account of what took place next is very similar to the record of the case held in the Exchequer Court, later published in *Fraser's Magazine*. Having gone to his club in London, Berkeley was able to establish the whereabouts of Fraser, the magazine's eponymous editor, from whom he sought clarification of the author's name and address. According to Berkeley he was accompanied only by his younger brother, Craven, who stationed himself inside the door of Fraser's Regent Street shop to prohibit interference from passers-by. In the court case Fraser's counsel tried to establish the existence of a hired thug who guarded the outside of the door (it appears from the court transcript that this thug was just a passer-by who wanted the fight to continue). Both accounts agree that Berkeley walked up to Fraser, who was alone in his office, and asked for the name and address of the author. Fraser, according to Berkeley's *Recollections*, refused to give up the information:

> This refusal of justice, with a full knowledge of the responsibility incurred by it, in my eyes warranted severe chastisement. I at once with my fist knocked him down on his desk, whence on his recovering he snatched at some weapon close behind him. I never knew what it was, but, seizing him by the collar, hurled him into the middle of his shop; where, on his refusing to rise, and on my brother handing me a racing-whip he had brought for my use, I gave him a severe flogging, which concluded in the gutter of the street, up which he presently fled, crying loudly for help.

At the trial Fraser's lawyers stressed the great size and strength of Berkeley in comparison to their client (despite the fact that in his *Recollections* Berkeley remembers Fraser as 'a man between thirty and forty, and apparently in the prime of life and strength') and the fact that a third person, a hired thug, was also present, barring the door from the outside. The description given in court was far more graphic than in Berkeley's *Recollections*, but neither counsel made any mention of a weapon in Fraser's hands:

> Mr Grantley Berkeley, unawares to Mr Fraser, clenched his fist, and struck him a violent blow on his right temple, which felled him flat to the ground.... and as he was endeavouring to rise, Mr Grantley Berkeley struck him down again; then, laying hold of his collar with his

left hand, with the clenched fist of his right hand he continued to strike him about the head, the face and every part of his body which came within reach; he then changed his weapon of torment [to a stout riding crop]… taking the small end of this whip in his hand, Mr Fraser still prostrate at his feet, he struck my client with the butt-end of it about the head, the back, and shoulders; the butt-end of the whip is described by a witness as being about the thickness of his thumb, the end of it bound with wire. With this blunt instrument did the defendant cut through the flesh of Mr Fraser's head, and laid it open… he then took the butt-end of the whip in his hand, and as Mr Fraser was still lying at his feet with his face exposed, he struck him over the head and face with the lash-end of it, – the very first blow, as I am told, fetching blood from the temple down to the chin… and by an effort of natural instinct he raised his hands to cover his eyes; and it was a most fortunate thing for him that this natural instinct came to his aid, because one of his hands when so placed was cut across the back, right through to the bone.

Both sources agree that the struggle ended outside of the shop in busy Regent's Street where a crowd, unfavourable to the Berkeleys, called a policeman to arrest them. They were led to Great Marlborough Street to see the sitting magistrate who, Grantley Berkeley complained, appeared to be immediately prejudiced against him, ordering him to put down the horsewhip which still dangled from his wrist (Grantley does not mention his brother's presence at court). After being granted bail Grantley Berkeley immediately set about finding the real target of his anger, William Maginn.

In the end it was Maginn who contacted Berkeley. Apparently, so enraged was Fraser by his beating that he threatened to have Maginn arrested for a personal debt if he did not shoot Berkeley. Maginn dropped off a card at Berkeley House, the family's London home, and a duel was arranged on a quiet spot along the Harrow Road a few miles outside the city. The duel was a farcical affair with both men displaying an incompetence with pistols that can scarcely have been equalled, despite Berkeley's boast that, 'Had we fought with my copper-cap John Manton pistols, that I was used to, I could have hit any button on my adversary's coat'. The two duellists stationed themselves only ten paces apart. Berkeley recalls the following series of events:

I awaited his discharge, and delivered mine immediately after, taking a hasty aim at his leg. The ball went through my pistol-case, at which he was standing, striking on the hinge of the lid, one moiety going into the heel of Dr Maginn's boot. He had very nearly as narrow escape from his own bullet, which in consequence of overhaste in pulling the trigger, buried itself close to his foot in the turf, to which the wadding set fire for a moment or two.

With Fraser egging them on, the weapons were reloaded:

> I again received my opponent's fire, and, after a slight delay, returned it. His ball ploughed up the ground within a yard of my right or left leg, I forget which, while mine passed close to him, rebounding from a slightly-rising ground in his rear... For a third time Major Fancourt loaded the weapons, and at the command to fire, Dr Maginn's third bullet ploughed up the turf about the same distance on the other side of me. On discharging mine, I thought he was seriously wounded, for something white appeared to fly from his breast, to which place he hurriedly raised his disengaged hand.

Maginn was escorted from the field but does not appear to have suffered any serious wound (interestingly, on 15 July 1842 Craven was also involved in a duel against a Captain Boldero over an insulting phrase which the captain had used against the queen, and both parties fired two shots to no effect). Fraser began court proceedings against Berkeley in the Exchequer Court in Michaelmas Term. A jury was convened and on 24 October 1836 the declaration of the plaintiff was made. The amount for which Fraser sued was £100 for medical bills and a huge £6,000 for damages. In the end the court agreed to the £100 for medical expenses only. Fraser immediately commenced fresh proceedings but in the end a settlement was reached: Fraser would accept the sum of £100 and in return Berkeley, who had launched a counter suit for the original libel, accepted forty shillings. In the same edition of *Fraser's Magazine* as the transcript of the trial appeared, Maginn wrote a short article in which he gave a defence of his and Fraser's actions.[10] He stated that,

> Mr Berkeley took what I shall ever consider to be a savage and cowardly revenge on Mr Fraser; and for half killing his victim, a jury awarded a fine of 100l. I have never heard but one opinion of that verdict. It appears to me to decide that a rich man may wreak his vengeance in any dastardly way he thinks fit, on any person who has offended him, at the expense of a mere trifle.

Eleven years after the exciting events following the publication of *Berkeley Castle*, the Berkeley-Lisle dispute was once again the inspiration for a piece of imaginative writing, this time an epic poem: *The Battle of Nibley Green*, by J.B. Kington. This was, if anything, even more creative with the facts than Grantley Berkeley's novel. The story takes place after the battle and centres around the character Hugh de Glanville, the king's commissioner, sent to enquire after the murder of Lisle. It opens with Lord Berkeley (called Earle Maurice!) sat brooding in a dark hall whilst relaxing in his chain mail. When the king's commissioner states his purpose, to look into the death of Lisle, the tormented 'earle' drags him to the dungeon and attempts to throw him down a deep shaft. The accuracy of the piece declines from hereon, reaching its nadir with the murder of a jester by Black Will, armed with a stool! From a purely historical context this poem is more interesting for its extended and thoroughly Whiggish preface which describes the state of law and order during the Wars of the Roses. This preface identifies weakness in central government as the cause of feuds such as that which culminated at Nibley Green, a theory with which many modern historians would concur. According to Kington, it is part of human nature to seek redress by violent means should legal ones fail, 'Private wars... are... a protest of the equitable sense, implanted in our human nature, against the tedium and practical deficiencies, or inapplicabilities of Law'; a sentiment with which Grantley Berkeley might have had some sympathy.

A generation later, in 1879, James Cooke published his account, and with him begins the modern, scholarly study of the Berkeley dispute, picking up, one might say, from where Smyth left off. But Cooke's work did not signal the end of Nibley Green's appearance in fiction. In 1881 W.S. Symonds, rector of Pendock, published *Malvern Chase: An Episode of the Wars of the Roses and the Battle of Tewkesbury. An Autobiography*. The hero gives a brief account of the battle. In a footnote Symonds gives as his source none other than J.H. Cooke.[11]

The battle of Nibley Green is still talked about in North Nibley, Berkeley and in the surrounding villages, and it has been described in several popular histories and guide books. However, the survival of the battle in popular memory and imagination owes considerably more to the careful scholarship of John Smyth, and the colourful fictions of Grantley Berkeley, than it does to the work of modern academic historians buried away in specialist monographs, PhD theses, and articles in learned journals. Perhaps this book will go some way towards bridging that divide.

Conclusion

The Berkeley dispute is a remarkable story – the stuff, indeed, of historical fiction – but what does it tell us about the attitudes and motivations of men and women in later medieval England? First of all, there are those themes which are familiar to any student of landed society and its disputes in this period. Quarrels were pursued through a combination of law suits, arbitration and direct, often violent, action. The law was not expected to deliver a definitive settlement nor to enforce its judgements unless the wronged party was ready and able to use a certain degree of muscle in the process. Violence certainly did occur, and to some degree was inevitable, but was usually contained within a framework of law and custom: there were rules to these rough games. Much of what we read in plaintiffs' testimony has to be taken with a pinch of salt: a court of law is not the place to hear the pure unvarnished truth. What lay behind many a tale of mayhem was probably no more than sabre-rattling: the show, rather than the implementation, of violence.

At Nibley Green, however, as elsewhere, the line of acceptable violence was most definitely crossed. Explaining how this came about has, we hope, been done. The question of why it happened still requires an answer. To some extent, we can blame the king, or rather, kings. At several points, in 1422, in 1450–51, and in 1469–71, we have seen how the dislocation of central authority – limited and short-lived in 1422, more serious on the other occasions – allowed tensions in the locality to burst through the usual constraints. With royal authority paralysed, disputants could seize their opportunity and try to grab what they could, in the hope that when order was restored, they would be allowed to keep at least some of their ill-gotten gains. Even effective kings at times appear, to modern eyes, to have acted against the interests of law and order. The granting of pardons, both general issues to anyone who wished to purchase them and to individuals, would seem to be the most blatant example of this. A contemporary might retort that, while the granting of a pardon was to some degree an admission of failure, and – looked at cynically – could be seen as putting the royal revenue before law-keeping, it was also part of Christian forgiveness, the lay version of remission of sin; but would Agnes Lewis have shared this opinion?

That there arose so many disputes to test the resources of medieval law-enforcement and kingship was partly the fault of the property law. In theory, the only person who actually owned land outright was the king; everyone else was his tenant, or a tenant of his tenant and so on down the feudal pyramid. Reality did not match up to this model however, and by the mid-fourteenth century various lawyer's stratagems had evolved to give landholders greater control over their estates. This produced a situation whereby in some cases the identity of the true owner of a particular piece of property was genuinely in doubt. The Berkeley entail is an example of such a legal device, but in this case there seems to have been little uncertainty about the fact of its existence. The creation of competing claims – by common law, by entail, and sometimes additionally by local customary law – provided ample opportunities for the greedy and unscrupulous to chance their arm.

Perhaps our protagonists were simply greedy and lacking in scruple, and we need look no further for an explanation than this. The main characters in the Berkeley drama were certainly not candidates for sainthood, but nor were they particularly exceptional for their time. What drove these people, and many of their contemporaries, to pursue their disputes so avidly, remorselessly even, and sometimes to the point of murder? Why did the Beauchamps and Talbots, to whose massive holdings the entailed Berkeley properties would have made only a marginal contribution, behave in this way?

Perhaps they enjoyed the chase. Litigation, the attempt to outwit one's opponent, might have a certain attraction to those with the money and time to pursue it, and the position and influence to give them reasonable protection from the consequences of losing. The use of direct action did allow for the exercise of some sort of martial skills: even if it entailed no more than terrorizing the opponent's tenantry, poaching his game, or cutting down his trees, there was at least the opportunity to wear armour, brandish weapons and ride about the countryside, pretending one was engaged in chivalric deeds of arms.

The chivalric mentality was certainly a factor in precipitating conflict at Nibley Green. The glorification of violence was combined with a heightened concept of honour. Having picked a fight, it was impossible to back down without loss of face, and loss of face might sometimes have been regarded as a greater calamity than loss of one's life. Perhaps the imperatives of the honour code forced disputants to persist beyond the point at which their efforts made any sense in terms of economic rationality. That the costs involved in pursuing a dispute – the expenditure, material damage and loss of life or limb – outweighed any likely material benefit to be gained by the victor was beside the point.

Personal honour was at stake, but so was the honour and well-being of the dynasty. Participants in these disputes were well aware that they were fighting not just for themselves and their immediate family, but for the benefit of their descendants and to redeem the sacrifices of their ancestors. Landed society thought in terms of lineage; its concept of family embraced each of the living, the dead and those yet to be born. The whole point of an entail like that created by Lord Berkeley in 1349 was that it would take effect after the death of its creator, and impose some sort of order on the lottery of birth, marriage and death. The return on a victory in something like the Berkeley dispute was to be calculated over a period of generations, not a single lifetime. The consensus held that the current head of a landed family could not treat the patrimony simply as his own property, with no thought to his heirs. His duty was to preserve, and if possible expand, that patrimony so that it would pass intact to the next generation. John Smyth understood this, which is why he was so outraged by the behaviour of William, marquis of Berkeley. William's brother Lord Maurice also understood this, which is why he spent his declining years haunting the law courts, doggedly reassembling his family's patrimony.

Our attempt to understand the Berkeley dispute should not be confined to the generalities of politics, the law, and aristocratic culture. The participants in these events were individual human beings. We can glimpse, or persuade ourselves that we can, their particular characters: the enigmatic Lord Thomas; Lord James, a courageous David faced with a succession of Goliaths; the impetuous young Viscount Lisle; the almost insanely obsessive Marquis William; and the quietly heroic – if perhaps equally obsessive – Lord Maurice. And then there is the female cast: women of iron will like Margaret, countess of Shrewsbury; the capable and ultimately tragic Isabel Mowbray; Margaret, Viscountess Lisle, possibly an even more tragic figure; and another victim in Agnes Lewis. The role of women as active and independent participants, as well as victims, in these struggles comes across very clearly. Much of the credit for the vividness of the characters and events rests with John Smyth, and here may lie a problem. No matter how careful we may be in interpreting the documentary evidence, Smyth's judgements are always present in the background, inevitably colouring our own portrayal. There is the additional problem of what may have been the participants' own attempts to manipulate the historical record, if our suspicions about the record of the events of January to March 1470 contained in the Berkeley Castle roll are correct. Inevitably, we are left with many questions. We can never know 'the truth' about Nibley Green, nor about any event or issue in history: each generation creates its own version of the truth, from John Smyth, to Grantley Berkeley, to ourselves.

Appendix

Viscount Lisle's Challenge and Lord Berkeley's Response, 1470

William called lord Berkeley, I marveill ye come not forth with all your Carts of gunnes, bowes, with oder ordinance, that ye set forward to come to my manor of Wotton to bete it down upon my head; I let you wit, ye shall not nede to come soe nye; for I trust to God to mete you nere home with English men of my one nation and neighbors, whereas ye by suttle craft have blowin about in divers places of England, That I should intend to bring in Welshmen for to destroy and hurt my one nation and Cuntry; I lete the wit, I was never soe disposed, nere never will bee; And to the proof hereof, I require thee of knighthood and of manhood to appoynt a day to meet me half way, there to try between God and our two hands, all our quarrell and title of right, for to eschew the shedding of Christian menns bloud, or els at the same day bringe the uttermost of thy power, and I shall mete thee; An answere of this by writinge, as ye will abide by, according to the honor and order of knighthood.

Thomas Talbot the Viscont Lisle.

Thomas Talbot, otherwise called viscont Lisle, not longe continued in that name but a new found thing brought out of Strange Contryes: I marveill greatly of thy strange and lewd writinge, made I suppose by thy false untrue Counsell that thou hast with thee, Hugh Mull, and Holt: As for Hugh Mull it is not unknown to all the worshipfull men of this Relme, how hee is attaynt of falseness and rasinge of the kings records; And as for the false mischevous Holt, what his rule hath be to the destruction of the kings lege pepull in my lordship of Berkeley, aswell to the hurt of their bodyes, as the losse of their goods, against Goddys lawe, consciens, and all reason, it is openly known, Soe that every worshipfull man should refuse to have them in his fellowship; And also of his own free will undesired of mee, before worshipfull and sufficient witnes, was sworn on a masse booke, That hee never should bee against mee in noe matter that I had a doe, and espetially in that untrue title that ye clayme, which ye hold my lyvelode with wrong; And where thou requirest mee of knighthood That I should appoynt a day and mete thee in the myd way between my manor of Wotton and my Castle of Berkeley, there to try betwyxt God and our two hands all our quarrell and title of right, for to eschewe the schedding of Christen mens bloud, or els the same day to bring the uttermost of my power, and thou would mete me; As for the determining betwixt our two hands of thy untrue clayme, and my title and right of my land and inheritance, thou wottest right well there is noe such determinac[i]on of land in this Relme used, And I ascertaine thee That my livelode, aswell my manor of Wotton as my Castle of Berkeley, be entayled to mee by fine of record in the kings Courts by the advice of all the Judges of this lond in that dayes being; And if it were soe That this matter might bee determined by thy honds and myne, the king our Soveraigne lord and his laws not offended, thou shouldst not so longe desire but I would assoone answere thee, in every poynt that belongeth to a knight: for thou art, God I take to record, in a false quarrell, and I in a true defence and title: And where thou desirest and requirest mee of knighthood and of manhood to appoynt a day, And that I should bee there with all the power that I could make, and that thou would mete mee half way, I will thou understand, I will not bring the tenth part that I can make, And I will appoint a short day to ease thy malitious hart and thy false Counsell that is with thee: faile not to morrow to be at Niblyes green at eight or nyne of the clock, And I will not faile with Gods might and grace to meete thee at the same place, the which standeth in the borders of the livelode that thou keepest untruly from me, redy to answere thee in all things, That I trust to God it shall be shewed on thee and thine to thy great shame and disworshipp: And remember, thy self and thy false Counsell have refused to abide the rule of the grete lordis of this lond, which by my will should have determyned this matter by thy evidences and mine, And therefore I vouch God to record and all the company of heaven, That this fact and the scheddinge of Christen mens bloud which shall be atwixt us two and our fellowshipps, if any hap to bee, doth grow of thy quaryll, and not of mee, but in my defence, and in eschewing of reproche, and onely through thy malitious and mischevouse purpose and of thy false Counsell, and of thy own simple discretion; And keepe thy day, And the trouth shall be shewed by the marcy of God.

William lord of Berkeley

From *Lives*, pp.109–11.

TABLE A

THE BERKELEYS, BEAUCHAMPS, TALBOTS AND GREYS

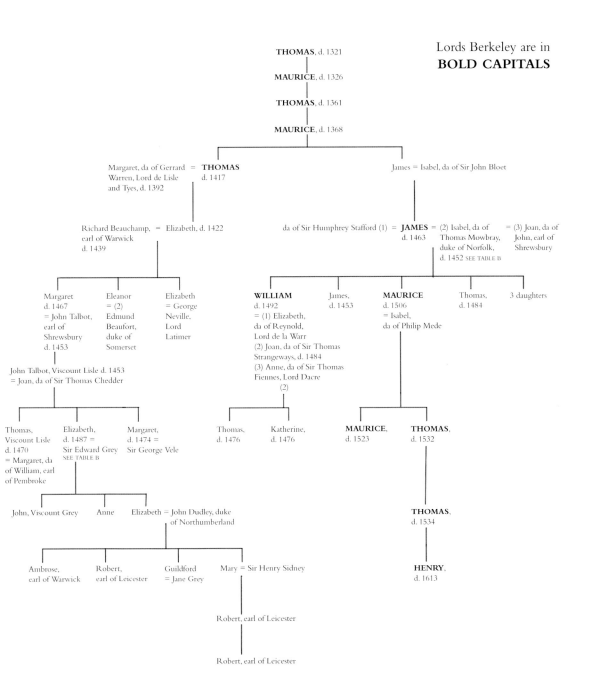

THOMAS, d. 1321

MAURICE, d. 1326

THOMAS, d. 1361

MAURICE, d. 1368

Lords Berkeley are in
BOLD CAPITALS

Margaret, da of Gerrard = **THOMAS**
Warren, Lord de Lisle   d. 1417
and Tyes, d. 1392

James = Isabel, da of Sir John Bloet

Richard Beauchamp, = Elizabeth, d. 1422
earl of Warwick
d. 1439

da of Sir Humphrey Stafford (1) = **JAMES** = (2) Isabel, da of   = (3) Joan, da of
                                     d. 1463   Thomas Mowbray,   John, earl of
                                                  duke of Norfolk,   Shrewsbury
                                                  d. 1452 SEE TABLE B

Margaret   Eleanor   Elizabeth
d. 1467   = (2)   = George
= John Talbot,   Edmund   Neville,
earl of   Beaufort,   Lord
Shrewsbury   duke of   Latimer
d. 1453   Somerset

WILLIAM   James,   **MAURICE**   Thomas,   3 daughters
d. 1492   d. 1453   d. 1506   d. 1484
= (1) Elizabeth,   = Isabel,
da of Reynold,   da of Philip Mede
Lord de la Warr
(2) Joan, da of Sir Thomas
Strangeways, d. 1484
(3) Anne, da of Sir Thomas
Fiennes, Lord Dacre
(2)

John Talbot, Viscount Lisle d. 1453
= Joan, da of Sir Thomas Chedder

Thomas,   Elizabeth,   Margaret,
Viscount Lisle   d. 1487 =   d. 1474 =
d. 1470   Sir Edward Grey Sir George Vele
= Margaret, da   SEE TABLE B
of William, earl
of Pembroke

Thomas,   Katherine,   **MAURICE**,   **THOMAS**,
d. 1476   d. 1476   d. 1523   d. 1532

John, Viscount Grey   Anne   Elizabeth = John Dudley, duke
                                          of Northumberland

THOMAS,
d. 1534

Ambrose,   Robert,   Guildford   Mary = Sir Henry Sidney
earl of Warwick earl of Leicester = Jane Grey

HENRY,
d. 1613

Robert, earl of Leicester

Robert, earl of Leicester

TABLE B

THE BERKELEYS, MOWBRAYS AND GREYS

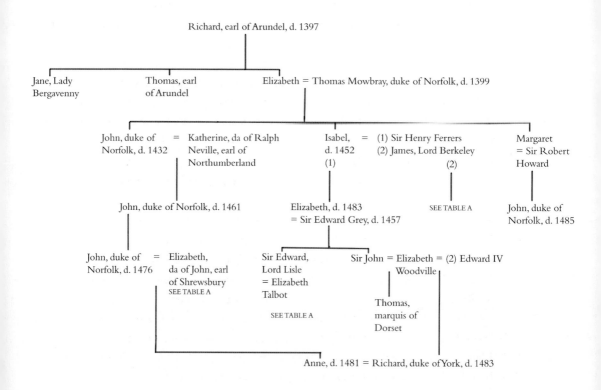

Richard, earl of Arundel, d. 1397

Jane, Lady Bergavenny   Thomas, earl of Arundel   Elizabeth = Thomas Mowbray, duke of Norfolk, d. 1399

John, duke of Norfolk, d. 1432 = Katherine, da of Ralph Neville, earl of Northumberland

Isabel, d. 1452 (1) = (1) Sir Henry Ferrers / (2) James, Lord Berkeley (2)

Margaret = Sir Robert Howard

John, duke of Norfolk, d. 1461

Elizabeth, d. 1483 = Sir Edward Grey, d. 1457

SEE TABLE A

John, duke of Norfolk, d. 1485

John, duke of Norfolk, d. 1476 = Elizabeth, da of John, earl of Shrewsbury
SEE TABLE A

Sir Edward, Lord Lisle = Elizabeth Talbot

SEE TABLE A

Sir John = Elizabeth = (2) Edward IV
Woodville

Thomas, marquis of Dorset

Anne, d. 1481 = Richard, duke of York, d. 1483

NOTES

INTRODUCTION

1. J.H. Cooke, 'The Berkeley MSS and their author, John Smyth', *TBGAS*, 5 (1880–81), pp.12–16; J. Maclean (ed.), *The Berkeley Manuscripts: The Lives of the Berkeleys*, vol. 1 (Bristol and Gloucestershire Archaeological Society, 1883), pp.2–3; A.T. Woollett, 'Myte and duty: John Smyth of Nibley and the lords of Berkeley, 1597–1641', unpublished University of Boston BA dissertation (1989) (copy in GRO).
2. Berkeley Castle was looted in 1645 by Parliamentarian forces, and many records destroyed: E.S. Lindley, 'A John Smyth bibliography', *TBGAS*, 80 (1961), pp.121–31, 122.
3. J.H. Cooke, 'The Great Berkeley Law-Suit of the 15th and 16th Centuries. A Chapter of Gloucestershire History', *TBGAS*, 3 (1878–9), pp.304–324; J.H. Cooke, *The Great Berkeley Law Suit of the Fifteenth and Sixteenth Centuries: a Chapter of Gloucestershire History* (Berkeley, 1879); J.H. Cooke, *A Sketch of the History of Berkeley its Castle, Church and The Berkeley Family* (Berkeley, 1879), reprinted in 1910 as *A Handbook for Visitors to Berkeley its Castle and Church with a Short Account of the Berkeley Family,* which sums up the book's contents well.
4. J. Maclean (ed.), *The Berkeley Manuscripts: The Lives of the Berkeleys*, 2 vols (Bristol and Gloucestershire Archaeological Society, 1883); *A Description of the Hundred of Berkeley* (Bristol and Gloucestershire Archaeological Society, 1885).
5. I.H. Jeayes, *Descriptive Catalogue of the Charters and Muniments… at Berkeley Castle* (Bristol, 1892).
6. T.A. Ryder, *Mid-Gloucestershire Thro' the Ages* (Worcester, 1951); J. Blow, 'Nibley Green, 1469', *History Today*, 2 (1952), pp.598–618, reprinted in C.M.D. Crowder (ed.), *English Society and Government in the Fifteenth Century* (London, 1967), pp.86–111, as 'Nibley Green 1470: the last private battle fought in England'.

1 – THE ROAD TO NIBLEY GREEN

1. The following is drawn from D. Walker (ed.), *The Cartulary of St Augustine's Abbey, Bristol*, (Bristol and Gloucestershire Archaeological Society, 1998), pp.xi–xiv.
2. The following is based on B. Harvey, 'The Berkeleys of Berkeley, 1281–1417: a study in the lesser peerage of late medieval England' unpublished University of St Andrew's PhD thesis (1990) (copy in GRO).
3. C. Dyer, *Standards of Living in the Later Middle Ages: Social Change in England, c.1200–1520* (Cambridge, 1989), p.31.
4. A. Sinclair, 'The great Berkeley law-suit revisited, 1417–39', *Southern History*, 9 (1987), pp.34–50, 35.
5. *Lives*, pp.4–5.
6. Details of the Lisle inheritance are given in A.F.J. Sinclair, 'The Beauchamp earls of Warwick in the Later Middle Ages', unpublished University of London PhD thesis (1987), p.363.
7. For Richard Beauchamp, earl of Warwick, see also Hicks, *Warwick, passim*, and 'Descent, partition and extinction: the Warwick inheritance' and 'The Beauchamp Trust, 1439–87', in his *Richard III and his Rivals: Magnates and their Motives in the Wars of the Roses* (London, 1991), pp.323–336, 337–352.
8. *Lives*, p.27.
9. Unless otherwise stated, the following is based on Sinclair, 'The great Berkeley law-suit revisited', *passim*.
10. Jeayes, *Catalogue*, p.182, no. 581.
11. *Lives*, p.36. At one point (p.40), Smyth refers to an agreement between Thomas and Sir John St John, made in April 1410, that James and Maurice should marry his daughters, but James's marriage, if it took place, was evidently short-lived, since Smyth then states that in July 1414 Thomas arranged his marriage to a daughter of Sir Humphrey Stafford of Hooke, Dorset, who brought with her a marriage portion of 600 marks. In both cases he is adamant that Thomas assured the brides' fathers that his nephew was heir to the entailed estates. Later (pp.79–80), Smyth writes as though the existence of the first marriage is in doubt.
12. *Lives*, p.36
13. Ibid., p.41.
14. Ibid., p.34; Jeayes, *Catalogue*, p.270.
15. *Calendar of Inquisitions Post Mortem*, vol. 20, *1413–1418* (London, 1995), no. 816.
16. The countess of Warwick had household expenses of between £800 and £1,000 in the year Michaelmas 1420 to Michaelmas 1421. The earl could spend five times that amount over the same period: C.D. Ross, 'The household accounts of

Elizabeth Berkeley, countess of Warwick, 1420–21', *TBGAS*, 70 (1951), pp.81–105, 84.

17. *Lives*, p.43

18. His negotiations about the siege of Berkeley Castle kept him in Gloucestershire until 20 September, when he was summoned to Windsor to discuss the ramifications of the king's death: Griffiths, *Henry VI*, p.12. The siege had presumably ended by then.

19. Here Smyth refers to the daughter of Sir Humphrey Stafford. Because they had no children, James was unable to keep her portion of 600 marks after her death: *Lives*, pp.48, 79.

20. Unless otherwise stated, the following is based on A.J. Pollard, 'The family of Talbot, Lords Talbot and earls of Shrewsbury in the fifteenth century', unpublished University of Bristol PhD thesis, 3 vols (1968), vol. 1, pp.38–51.

21. *Lives*, p.80.

22. The feoffees are named in a later enfeoffment made by Thomas, 2nd Lord Stanley, in 1466: PRO E326/512.

23. Griffiths, *Henry VI*, pp.37, 141, 161.

24. *Lives*, p.80.

25. *Lives*, p.100; Griffiths, *Henry VI*, p.279. G. Waters, 'William, Lord Berkeley', in J. Petre (ed.), *Richard III: Crown and People* (Gloucester, 1985), pp.69–78, is a concise biography.

26. Hicks, *Warwick*, p.78.

27. *Lives*, p.59.

28. Hicks, *Warwick*, pp.40, 46.

29. Hicks, *Warwick*, pp.46–7; *CPR, 1446–52*, pp.432–3.

30. *Lives*, p.73.

31. *Lives*, pp.62–3.

32. *Lives*, p.77; Pollard, 'The family of Talbot', vol. 3, p.420; Sinclair, 'Beauchamp earls of Warwick', p.329.

33. *Lives*, pp.64–71, 102–3, 117; PRO C1/66/105. A John Wenlock of Blackmere, Shropshire, had been retained by the countess of Shrewsbury from at least 1442, presumably the same man: Pollard, 'The family of Talbot', vol. 3, p.419.

34. See below, pp.78, 82–3.

35. PRO KB27/763/41–2, cited in Pollard, 'The family of Talbot', vol. 1, p.47.

36. PRO E326/3358. The other witness was John Bradstone: Pollard, 'The family of Talbot', vol. 3, p.419.

37. *Lives*, p.71. Pollard, 'The family of Talbot', vol. 3, p.420.

38. *Lives*, p.82.

39. The following is based on *Lives*, pp.75–6, 81–2.

40. Hicks, *Warwick*, p.225.

41. The following is based on *Lives*, pp.104–7.

42. Judging by the pardon granted to William in March 1465 for all entrances and intrusions into Berkeley Castle, manor and lordship after the death of his father: *CPR, 1461–67*, p.289.

43. For Viscount Lisle's inheritance, see *Lives*, pp.106, 125. A copy of Margaret's inquisition *post mortem*, held at Gloucester on 28 October 1467, names Thomas Talbot, aged nineteen or more, as her heir: GRO D18/175. After his death writs of *diem clausit extremum* were sent to escheators of Middlesex, Berkshire, Wiltshire, Gloucestershire and the March, Staffordshire, Warwickshire, Worcestershire, Somerset, Devon and Bristol: *CFR, 1461–71*, p.260.

44. *CPR 1461–67*, pp.41, 49; G.E.C., *Complete Peerage*, vol. 8 (London, 1932), p.58; D. Thomas, 'The Herberts of Raglan as supporters of the house of York in the second half of the fifteenth century', unpublished University of Wales (Cardiff) MA thesis (1967), p.96. See Hicks, *Clarence*, p.26, and Ross, *Edward IV*, p.77, for the political connections of Lord Herbert.

45. This was certainly Smyth's opinion: *Lives*, pp.106–7.

2   THE BATTLE

1. The following is based on *Lives*, pp.107–111.

2. Berkeley Castle Muniments, Select Roll 137: Jeayes, *Catalogue*, p.298.

3. PRO E326/475.

4. See Appendix for the text of the challenge and response. The battle of Nibley Green took place less than a year after the completion of Sir Thomas Malory's great work, usually known as the *Morte Darthur*; Malory's style and that of the texts' composers show striking similarities, suggesting a shared cultural milieu: E.Vinaver (ed.), *Malory: Works* (2nd edn, Oxford, 1971), p.726; P.J.C. Field, *The Life and Times of Sir Thomas Malory* (Woodbridge, 1993).

5. C. Given-Wilson, *The English Nobility in the Late Middle Ages* (London, 1987), p.48.

6. See below, pp.97, 101.

7. R.R. Davies, *The Revolt of Owain Glyn Dŵr* (Oxford, 1995), *passim*.

8. Griffiths, *Henry VI*, p.168.

9. H.T. Evans, *Wales and the Wars of the Roses* (1998 edn, Stroud), pp.41–110; Thomas, 'The Herberts of Raglan', *passim*.

10. Sinclair, 'The great Berkeley law-suit revisited', p.44.

11. For discussion of these issues see R.W. Kaeuper, *Chivalry and Violence in Medieval*

Europe (Oxford, 1999), and the essays in Kaeuper (ed.), *Violence in Medieval Society* (Woodbridge, 2000).

12. M.H. Keen, *The Laws of War in the Late Middle Ages* (London, 1965), pp.40–44; M. Vale, 'Aristocratic violence: trial by battle in the Later Middle Ages', in Kaeuper (ed.), *Violence in Medieval Society*, pp.159–82; J. Huizinga, *Homo Ludens: A Study of the Play Element in Culture* (London, 1970), pp.114–7.

13. This is perhaps a disingenuous reference to the settlement of 1463, which William probably opposed.

14. The following is based on M. Hicks, 'Idealism in Late Medieval English Politics', in Hicks, *Richard III and His Rivals*, pp.41–59.

15. PRO E326/3358

16. PRO KB27/841 mm 81, 85; 840 mm 8, 18; 842 mm 75–6; 844 m 23, rex m 38d.

17. *Lives*, pp.147–8.

18. GRO D1677/GG 245, 253, 256, 272–3, 275, 284, 346a, D2244/135, 150–1, 202; CPR, 1476–85, p.384. For Leland see below, p.66.

19. BL Add Ch 72,687.

20. Wedgwood, *History of Parliament*, p.54; Carpenter, *Locality and Polity*, *passim*.

21. Berkeley Castle Muniments, Select Charters, 625: Jeayes, *Catalogue*, pp.191–2; *Lives*, pp.113–4.

22. L.T. Smith (ed.), *The Itinerary of John Leland in or about the years 1535–1543, Part 8* (London, 1909), pp.105, 132.

23. *Camden's Britannia, 1695: A Facsimile of the 1695 Edition Published by Edmund Gibson* (Newton Abbot, 1971), p.238 n. 13.

24. The following is based on *Lives*, pp.114–5.

25. The following is based on D. Tandy, *And Did Those Feet... A Survey of Alkington for the Year 2001* (privately printed, 2001); H.P.R. Finberg, *Gloucestershire Studies* (Leicester, 1957), pp.148–9; and J.M. Popplewell, 'North Nibley: a study in settlement and land use in a south Gloucestershire parish', unpublished University of Bristol MA dissertation (1982).

26. A.W. Boardman, *The Medieval Soldier in the Wars of the Roses* (Stroud, 1998), pp.143–8.

27. Ibid., pp.129–31.

28. Ibid., p.167.

29. The wording on the patent roll (PRO C66/527 m. 8) is ambiguous, but Daunt was clearly a Lisle follower, putting Lewis on the side of Berkeley.

30. *Lives*, p.113.

31. Ibid., p.115.

3 – AFTERMATH

1. For events in this and the following paragraph, see Ross, *Edward IV*, pp.126–160, and Hicks, *Warwick*, pp.271–296.
2. *Lives*, p.111.
3. A. Goodman, *The Wars of the Roses: Military Activity and English Society, 1452–1497* (London, 1981), p.222.
4. *Lives*, pp.96–7; Smith, *Itinerary of John Leland… Part 8*, p.105.
5. Wedgwood, *History of Parliament*, p.261; *Lives*, p.117; Smyth, *History of the Hundred of Berkeley*, pp.311, 406; Pollard, 'The Family of Talbot', vol. 2, p.419. GRO D2930/3, pp.19–20.
6. *CPR, 1461–67*, p.101.
7. P.W. Hammond, *The Battles of Barnet and Tewkesbury* (Gloucester, 1990), p.81; *Gloucestershire Notes & Queries*, 1 (1885), p.280; Wedgwood, *History of Parliament*, p.261.
8. *CFR, 1461–71*, p.260; *CCR, 1468–76*, no. 538; *CPR, 1467–77*, p.305; PRO C140/35/58. Grey was the grandchild of Lord Berkeley's mother Isabel Mowbray by Henry, Lord Ferrers of Groby, and the brother-in-law of Elizabeth Woodville. For the Talbot sisters' marriages and their husbands, see L.E. Moye, 'The estates and finances of the Mowbray family, earls marshal and dukes of Norfolk, 1401–1476', unpublished Duke University PhD thesis (1985), p.217 (copy in GRO); Hicks, *Warwick*, pp.222, 224, 252, 286, 297.
9. He also sat on the Somerset bench from June 1476: *CPR, 1467–77*, pp.614, 628–9.
10. This excludes senior ecclesiastics and great magnates appointed to numerous commissions, but not expected to sit on them all, and JPs of the quorum, professional judges who were appointed to commissions to lend their expertise. The other two were Sir Ralph Boteler of Sudeley, who was dead by May 1473, and so was probably unfit to serve (*CFR, 1471–85*, no. 158); and John Huggeford, who continued as a Warwickshire JP (Wedgwood, *History of Parliament*, pp.478–9).
11. J.R. Lander, *English Justices of the Peace, 1461–1509* (Gloucester, 1989), pp.109–112, 120–24, 139. William Berkeley of Weoley in Worcestershire, by comparison, who was also a supporter of the Readeption regime, served continuously on his county bench from January 1471 until February 1473: *CPR, 1467–77*, p.636.
12. *CPR, 1467–77*, p.303; PRO C67/49 m 22. On 20 June 1472 the sheriff of Gloucestershire was notified by letter patent of Lord Berkeley's pardon: Jeayes, *Catalogue*, p.195, no. 638.
13. *CPR, 1467–77*, p.429.

14. *Lives*, pp.148, 154.

15. W.H. Dunham, *Lord Hastings' Indentured Retainers, 1461–83*, Transactions of the Connecticut Academy of Arts and Sciences, 39 (1955), pp.118–9, 125, 141; *Lives*, p.135. The near contemporary list of those knighted at Tewkesbury mistakenly identifies the Maurice Berkeley knighted at the battle with Lord Berkeley's brother. This Sir Maurice is almost certainly Sir Maurice Berkeley of Beverstone, Gloucestershire, one of Edward IV's squires of the body who had accompanied him into exile: J. Gairdner (ed.), *The Paston Letters*, vol. 5 (Stroud, 1986), p.105 ('Sir Moreys of Barkley'); Wedgwood, *History of Parliament*, pp.67–8; PRO E404 73/3/45, 74/1/134, 75/1/46, 75/2/10 (for Maurice, squire, then knight of the body); C67/48 m. 11 (for his pardon, 1472).

16. Smith, *Itinerary of John Leland… Part 8*, p.105.

17. *CPR, 1467–77*, p.219. On 25 May Lord Berkeley purchased a royal pardon, but this only covered offences committed before Christmas 1469, so it would not have covered Lisle's death: *Lives*, p.136.

18. *CPR, 1467–77*, pp.251, 614.

19. Ross, *Edward IV*, pp.155–8; Hicks, *Warwick*, pp.303–4.

20. Hammond, *The Battles of Barnet and Tewkesbury*, pp.81–6, 95.

21. *CPR, 1461–67*, pp.117, 434. *CFR, 1461–71*, p.231; M. Hicks, 'Edward IV, the Duke of Somerset and Lancastrian Loyalism in the North', in his *Richard III and His Rivals*, pp.149–63, 153–4.

22. Just who held St Briavel's Castle is unclear, but both Clarence and Warwick clearly had great influence in the area: N.M. Herbert (ed.), *Victoria History of the County of Gloucester*, vol. 5 (Oxford, 1996), pp.256, 414; R.A. Brown, H.M. Colvin, A.J. Taylor, *The History of the Kings Works*, vol. 2 (London, 1963), p.823; W. Taprell Allen, 'St Briavel's Castle', *TBGAS*, 3 (1878–9), pp.325–50; Hicks, *Clarence,* pp.81–2.

23. Hicks, *Clarence,* p.37.

24. Ibid., p.48; PRO KB27/836 m. 61d.

25. Carpenter, *Locality and Polity*, pp.492, 500, 510. Sir William Berkeley of Weoley, Worcestershire, and Stoke, Gloucestershire, was pardoned for his participation in the Readeption in December 1471: *CPR, 1467–77*, p.303.

26. *CPR 1467–77*, pp.484, 490, 495; *CPR, 1476–85*, p.24; PRO C67/48 m. 26, where in his pardon he is described as James of Lydney esquire, alias gentleman.

27. For Cassey and his family see J.N. Langsten, 'Old Catholic families of Gloucestershire: the Casseys of Wightfield in Deerhurst', *TBGAS*, 74 (1955), pp.128–52, 134–5; Pollard, 'Family of Talbot', vol. 2, p.419. John and William Cassey, sons of John Cassey esquire of Wightfield, appear in a deed of 1483: GRO D214 T9.

28. *CPR, 1467–77*, p.614; *CFR, 1461–71*, nos 254, 255, 268, 269; *CCR, 1468–76*, no. 525.

29. *CPR, 1467–77*, pp.349, 407, 453, 614; *CCR, 1468–76*, no. 525. In 1477 John Cassey appeared as a feoffee with Sir Richard Beauchamp of Powicke, and the following year he joined Maurice Berkeley and John Twynyho on a commission of enquiry into Clarence's property in Gloucestershire: *CPR, 1476–85*, pp.44, 109. Cassey appeared as a witness to the re-enfeoffment of Berkeley Castle in March 1472: PRO E326/475. He died in 1483: *CFR, 1471–85*, no. 738. For Twynyho see Hicks, *Clarence*, pp.125, 150, 162, 200, 202. Twynyho's will of 1485 mentions a silver goblet, 'which the venerable duke of Clarence from his benevolence gave to me': PRO PROB 11/7 f. 14. John Twynyho was one of the Berkeley feoffees appointed in May 1466 and re-appointed in March 1472: 1466, PRO E326/512 (another copy of the deed is calendered in Jeayes, *Catalogue*, p.189, no. 614); 1472, PRO E326/475.

30. Hicks, *Clarence*, pp.120, 138–9; Hicks, *Warwick*, pp.120, 138–9; Wedgwood, *History of Parliament*, p.54.

31. Hammond, *Barnet and Tewkesbury*, p.84; Thomas, 'Herberts of Raglan', pp.245–6. J.O. Halliwell (ed.), *A Chronicle of the First Thirteen Years of the Reign of King Edward the Fourth by John Warkworth, D.D.*, Camden Society (1839), p.7; J. Bruce (ed.), *Historie of the Arrivall of Edward IV. in England and the Final Recouerye of his Kingdomes from Henry VI. A.D. M.CCCC.LXXI*, Camden Society (1838), pp.25–6, both reprinted, with original pagination, and introduction by K. Dockray, in *Three Chronicles of the Reign of Edward IV* (Gloucester, 1988).

32. The following is based on F.B. Bickley (ed.), *The Little Red Book of Bristol*, 2 vols (Bristol, 1900), vol. 2, pp.130–2; E.W.W. Veale (ed.), *The Great Red Book of Bristol: Text pt. 4*, Bristol Record Society, 18 (1953), pp.57–8, 69–70, 81–2; *CCR, 1468–1476*, no. 843.

33. *CPR, 1461–67*, pp.490–1.

34. The feoffees appointed in May 1466 are given in PRO E326/512; those remaining and those newly appointed in March 1472 in PRO E326/475.

35. Hicks, *Warwick*, p.185; Carpenter, *Locality and Polity*, pp.230–1, 484 n. 159, 500 n. 53, 524, 656, 686, 697, 700; Sinclair, 'Great Berkeley law suit', p.39.

36. P.R. Coss (ed.), *The Langley Cartulary*, Dugdale Society, 32 (1980), p.40.

37. Wedgwood, *History of Parliament*, pp.67–9, confuses William Berkeley of Uley, Gloucestershire, with William Berkeley of Weoley, Worcestershire, who was a supporter of the Readeption.

38. Hicks, *Clarence*, pp.51, 55, 60, 72–3, 75–6, 77 n. 115, 88; Hicks, *Warwick*, pp.287, 300; Wedgwood, *History of Parliament*, pp.473–4, 799–800, 955–6; *Dictionary of National Biography*, vol. 28, pp.42–3, vol. 54, pp.81–2; M.K. Jones, 'Sir William

Stanley of Holt: politics and family allegiance in the late fifteenth century', *Welsh History Review*, 14 (1988), pp.1–22.

39. For which, see Hicks, *Clarence*, pp.190, 192–3.

40. PRO KB27/841 mm 81, 85; 840 mm 8, 18; 842, mm 75–6; 844 m 23, rex m 38d; *Lives*, p.112. In March 1472, in order to support his claim that Berkeley Hundred was a liberty, Lord Berkeley obtained copies of old charters granting this privilege: Jeayes, *Catalogue*, p.192, nos 627, 628.

41. *Lives*, pp.142–3. Joan, daughter of Sir William Willoughby, was William's second wife. His first wife, Elizabeth, daughter of Reginald, Lord Delawarr, was divorced from him in 1467, raising suspicions that his second marriage was bigamous, and his children illegitimate: *Lives*, pp.138–42; Hereford and Worcester Record Office, 716.093/2648/6b iii (Register of Bishop John Carpenter, vol. 2), mm 224–226v.

42. *Lives*, p.112. The petition is PRO: SC8/122, no. 6089; for the bill and Act see *Rotuli Parliamentorum*, vol. 6, pp.205–7, and PRO C49/36/13.

43. Her last appearance in King's Bench was in Trinity Term, June 1472: KB 27/844 m 23. Negotiations would have begun before the start of the following term, Michaelmas, on 9 October.

44. Jeayes, *Catalogue*, p.193, no. 629; *Lives*, p.113; Ross, *Edward IV*, pp.410–11.

45. This and the following paragraph are based on PRO KB27/839 m 43, 840 mm. 8, 18, 841 m 28, 842 mm 75–6, 846 m 11; KB29/102 m 34r; C66/527 m. 8; C67/49, mm. 15–16; *CPR, 1467–77*, p.276.

4: RESOLUTION

1. *Lives*, p.143.

2. The other sister, Margaret, wife of Sir George Vere, had died without issue in 1474: *Lives*, p.115.

3. Ibid., p.116.

4. PRO C1/66/105; Jeayes, *Catalogue*, p.245, nos 847–9. Among others accused of involvement by the Berkeleys were John and Nicholas Daunt: see above, pp.44–5.

5. *Lives*, p.116.

6. PRO C1/100/62.

7. A. Crawford, 'The Mowbray inheritance', in J. Petre (ed.), *Richard III: Crown and People* (Gloucester, 1985), pp.79–85; P. Jones, 'Anne Mowbray', in ibid., pp.86–9.

8. *Rotuli Parliamentorum*, vol. 6, pp.205–207; Moye, 'Mowbray family', p.221.

9. Writhe's Book of Knights, BL Add. MSS. 46354, ff. 64–64b.

10. *Lives*, p.120.

11. Ibid., pp.126–7, 136; Jeayes, *Catalogue*, pp.195–6, nos 641–2, 644; *CCR, 1476–85*, nos 1225, 1263, 1353.

12. *Lives*, p.127.

13. Ibid., pp.127–8.

14. Jeayes, *Catalogue*, p.196, no. 643; *CCR, 1483–1500*, no. 28.

15. *Lives*, p.173.

16. Ibid., pp.155, 211, for the brothers' amicable relations up to 1484.

17. Smith, *Itinerary of John Leland... Part 8*, p.105.

18. Jeayes, *Catalogue*, p.198, no. 653; *Calendar of Charter Rolls, 1427–1516*, p.268; *CCR, 1485–1500*, nos 293–4.

19. PRO E41/199. For Edward Willoughby as a Berkeley feoffee, see Jeayes, *Catalogue*, pp.196–7, nos 646, 648–50. For Bray and Willoughby, see S.B. Chrimes, *Henry VII* (London, 1972), pp.58, 110.

20. *Lives*, pp.131–2; Jeayes, *Catalogue*, pp.198–9, nos 656–7.

21. Ibid., pp.197–8, nos 652, 654.

22. PRO LR 14/87. Berkeley's will: PROB 11/9, mm. 88–9; *Lives*, pp.iii–vi. The Elizabethan antiquarian John Stow noted the tombs of William and Joan in St Augustine's Friary, but after the Dissolution the friary was given to the marquis of Winchester, who converted it into a town house. The church was reserved for London's Dutch community; but his son sold 'the monuments of noblemen, buried there, for one hundred pounds': C.L. Kingsford (ed.), *A Survey of London by John Stow*, vol. 1 (Oxford, 1908), pp.177–9; P. Cunningham, *A Handbook of London Past and Present*, 2nd edn (East Ardsley, 1978), p.26.

23. William Berkeley's year of death is often given as 1491, following *Lives*, p.146. His will was dated 5 February 'the yere of our Lord god' 1491, the seventh regnal year of Henry VII (which ran from 22 August 1491 to 21 August 1492; Smyth also gives this regnal year), and probate was granted on 6 April 1492. At this time the year of grace ran from Lady Day (25 March) to Lady Day, so by fifteenth-century reckoning February, 7 Henry VII fell in 1491, but by modern reckoning this is 1492. The bill for painting the various armorial displays and banners for Lord Berkeley's funeral came to £23 2s. 4d.: BL Stowe MSS 1047 f. 220b (which also gives his time of death as the night of 14 February), Add MSS 45131, ff. 23–23b, 46354 f. 62b.

24. *Lives*, p.145. The present Wotton Manor – for most of its life the vicarage to the adjacent parish church – was begun in 1610 on the foundations of the medieval house, from which some building materials were reclaimed. We are grateful to Mr Mark Jones, of the Manor House, for this information.

25. Ibid., p.191.

26. The following based on Cooke, 'Great Berkeley Law Suit', pp.320–24.

5: The Myth of Nibley Green

1. *The Ancient and Present State of Gloucestershire* (York, 1974); *A New History of Gloucestershire* (Dursley, 1977). Both works have had a major influence on later Gloucestershire historians. According to Finberg, they 'dominate all other histories of the county': *Gloucestershire Studies* (Leicester, 1957), p.277.

2. The figure of 150 dead has often been repeated, and may in some way explain Jonathan Blow's statement in his 1952 *History Today* article, 'That casualties were considerable we have learned from the excavation in Victorian times of the large communal grave by Nibley Church, in which a hundred and fifty skeletons were found'. Blow's article was not footnoted, and any record of this excavation has so far eluded us: 'Nibley Green, 1469', *History Today*, 2 (1952), pp.598–618. We are grateful to the Gloucestershire Museums Service and the Gloucestershire Sites and Monuments Record for help on this point.

3. T.D. Fosbrooke, *The Berkeley Manuscripts: Abstracts and Extracts of Smyth's Lives of the Berkeleys* (London, 1821), p.v.

4. *Berkeley Castle: An Historical Romance*, 3 vols (London, 1836). The publisher's contract, dated 4 May 1836, is BL Add MSS 46612, and stands in stark contrast to the modern equivalent: Richard Bentley, of New Burlington Street, London, agreed to publish 'a work of fiction written by the said Honourable Grantley Berkley [*sic*] MP entitled "Berkley [*sic*] Castle" forming three volumes & of the usual number of pages in each volume'.

5. W. Maginn, 'Mr Grantley Berkeley and his Novel', *Fraser's Magazine for Town and Country*, 14 (July–December, 1836), pp.242–7.

6. 'Fraser v. Berkeley and Another and Berkeley v. Fraser', *Fraser's Magazine for Town and Country*, 15 (January–June, 1837), pp.100–137.

7. *My Life and Recollections*, vol. 2 (London, 1865), Chapter 3, 'Authors and Critics', pp.43–84.

8. Mary's version of events is presented in Mary Tudor, *The Bxxxxxxx Family: a Narrative* (London, ?1822).

9. *Minutes of Evidence given before the Committee of Privileges to whom the Petition of William Fitzhardinge Berkeley, claiming as right to be Earl of Berkeley was referred*, 2 vols (London, 1811); *Dictionary of National Biography*, vol. 2, pp.342–3.

10. 'Defence of Fraser's Magazine in the Berkeley Affair', *Fraser's Magazine for Town and Country*, 15 (January–June 1837), pp.137–143.

11. We owe this reference to the kindness of Mr James Gough.

INDEX